S.1895

Susanne von Dietze

BALANCE
IN MOVEMENT

THE SEAT OF THE RIDER

J.A.Allen

To my mother,
who guided my eyes in the right direction.

British Library Cataloguing-in-Publication Data.
A catalogue record for this book is available from the British Library.

ISBN 0.85131.746.4

First published in Germany by FN-Verlag Reiterlichen Vereinigung GmbH,
Warendorf 1993

Second edition 1994

Published in Great Britain in 1999 by
J. A. Allen,
Clerkenwell House, 45–47 Clerkenwell Green,
London, EC1R 0HT

Typeset by Textype Typesetters, Cambridge
Film origination by Tenon & Polert Colour Scanning Ltd.
Printed by Dah Hua International Printing Press Co. Ltd., Hong Kong

Illustrations by Rudolf Strecker, Sassenberg
Designed by Nancy Lawrence

Contents

Foreword to English Language Edition

The time spent reading this book has been worth every moment. It contains so much material that has never been written about before and in areas that will help many people to ride, train and teach very much better.

The depth of detail means that to read *Balance in Movement* may take more concentration and time than horse people are normally willing to give up away from stables, fences and arenas. If they do, however, it is likely that they will find that many of the obstacles that lay in the way of them or their pupils acquiring a balanced secure seat can be removed.

One has wondered what lay behind the switch towards so much more sympathetic and harmonic riding in Germany in recent years. Knowledge as to how to achieve this way of riding, as contained in this book, must be one of them.

Jane Kidd

Foreword

'Anyone with the desire to become a better rider needs to know and understand their own body before being able to control it. Herein lies the hidden key to the rider's feel.' These words written by the author illustrate the intent of this book.

The secret of a good seat lies in the combination of seat and influence. The goal is the harmonious exterior form in combination with a barely visible feeling of communication between rider and horse. The skilful, sensitive and effortless communication between the rider and his horse we summarise under the term 'the feel of the rider'. It is the climax of all equestrian skills.

The term 'feel' refers to a seemingly inaccessible area. However, science has proven in the last few years that sensory achievements can and has to be learned. Therefore, the feel of the rider is not a gift that a rider possesses naturally, it is developed gradually through sensitive perceptions and corresponding reactions. Highly sensitive trainers will be especially successful with their students.

In this book Susanne von Dietze explores the 'classical seat' of the rider with the trained eye of a physiotherapist and an amateur riding instructor. The process she imparts to the reader is a surprising, perhaps even astonishing insight of how ingeniously tailored the prescribed requirements of the traditional riding system are with regard to the seat of the rider and the human body.

The author never suggests a static and externally idealistic form. She understands the interplay of the horse's back and the rider's weight at any given moment as balanced movement. She appeals for improved knowledge of the body, its perception and control. One's own sensitivity must be trained in order to develop the rider's feel, independent of the respective level of equestrian skill.

This book is a supplement to the *Richtlinien für Reiten und Fahren* (*Guidelines for Riding and Driving*), volume 1 and 2, as well as of *Sportlehre: Lernen, Lehren und Trainieren im Pferdesport* (*Sport Science: Learning, Teaching and Training in the Equestrian Sport*). It should become required reading for instructors and advanced riders.

Christoph Hess
Deutsche Reiterliche Vereinigung e.V.
Bereich Sport – Abteilung Ausbildung
(German Equestrian Federation, division sport
– department for training and education)

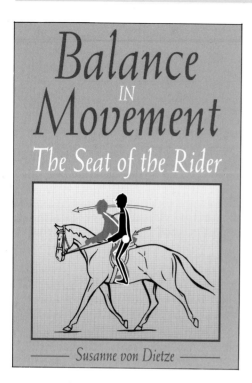

Balance
IN
Movement
The Seat of the Rider

——— Susanne von Dietze ———

Another book about riding?
Another book about riding!

There are already many books about riding. And to make matters worse, a book appears to be a difficult medium in which to approach the concept of riding. A book is a rigid theory and riding is about movement and dynamics. The balance that is required to sit on a horse is unthinkable without movement. Just imagine a bicyclist trying to maintain his balance in slow motion in front of a red traffic light. As soon as he comes to a stop he must put a foot down to save his equilibrium. Balance is possible only when in motion.

Movement has fascinated me, especially the harmony of movement, and the beauty of it. From afar I recognised humans for their typical body movements, not their faces. In my own riding practise, the harmonious movement of horse and rider was a more important goal than success at competitions. Then my profession taught me to analyse and understand movement, for a physiotherapist is also a kinetotherapist.

Soon I realised how difficult ordinary daily movements are to execute when one muscle or one joint does not work properly. It is the task of a physiotherapist to teach a patient individually-designed and efficient movements. Many of these movements happen instinctively and subconsciously. It is a difficult challenge to learn such behavioural movement. The physiotherapist always orients herself on the healthy movement. This is natural, functional and easy on the body. During my education and professional experience my eye was continually trained for all kinds of movement. So, I learned to understand riding as a movement as well, and I became interested as to how this movement works and how it can be learned.

My own riding education took place under the most favourable circumstances. I grew up in a family of riders with a small private breeding programme. I sat on the back of a horse before I learned how to walk. I did not acquire problems which often surface in the development of a young rider: I learned how to ride early enough, had good and diversified horse material, and was in exceptionally good hands, technically as well as pedagogically. All things considered, I could have become a very successful Young Rider. However, at the onset of puberty, I grew extremely tall and soon reached my considerable permanent height of 1.80 metres (5 feet 11 inches). With it came the breakdown of my riding. Horses, who went on the bit for me as a matter of course, suddenly turned into giraffes; I lost my natural feel on horseback, became frightened quickly and therefore often landed in the dirt. I owe it to the patience of my parents and some very special horses and ponies that I stuck to riding in spite of all this.

My mother always stressed the importance of the correct seat in my education. So I learned little by little to regain my quiet attitude on the back of a horse, in spite of my long and lanky arms and legs. However, fine coordination and thus effective influence on the horse remained a problem for a long time.

In the course of my training as a physiotherapist, my riding improved by leaps and bounds. Parallel to the better understanding of human anatomy, I learned to understand my own body better. This enabled me to work on the weaknesses of my movements and body position, to control them and thus rider better. I realised that the basics of physiotherapy are transferable to the seat of the rider. I completed an additional course of hippotherapy, the treatment of patients on horseback. In this therapy the movement of the horse is utilised to develop natural and healthy movement.

After finishing my education as an amateur riding instructor, my riding career continued for a while as a trainer in a dressage yard. The active exchange of ideas amongst professional and amateur trainers, as well as my own development, made it clear how little is being taught about the problem of learning how to ride – and simply for the reason that so little is known about it.

There exists in general a huge discrepancy between the training of the horse and that of a rider. As far as the horse is concerned, we are largely in agreement. The basic steps of training are laid down in the 'scales of training'. There exist plenty of concepts on how to build up the muscular system of a horse or how to correct wrong movement.

With regard to the rider we refer solely to the rigid ideal picture of the master. Compared to this, all deviations can only be registered as mistakes. A generally binding step-by-step guideline is non existent. Even the experts argue whether to first teach riding with or without stirrups, rising trot or sitting trot, 'head up' or 'heels down'.

Since the choice between my two professions was very difficult for me, I eventually realised them both: half the day I worked in a physiotherapy clinic with emphasis on 'spine' and the remainder I spent in a riding stable. There I taught beginners, both children and adults, treated hippotherapy patients and devoted myself increasingly to the development of the seat for advanced riders. Through this I tied together two apparently distant ends of my two professions and concluded: the knot stays put!

To look at facts from a different perspective often leads to new understanding.

From an extensive horse-related journey to Australia I brought a very special world map. From our point of view, it is upside down, with Australia located right in the middle. It is astounding how completely different the whole world can look, without falsifying the geography.

It is equally astounding how some

*It is astounding how completely different the whole world can look,
when 'turning it upside down'*

centres of gravity will shift, when one has the courage to put things upside down. I found an abundance of 'aha'-experiences once I looked at the classical way of riding, which I had learned from an early age, through the eyes of a physiotherapist. Many facts started to become really clear to me.

Riding is a complete and complex sport, which remains natural in all required movements. No unnatural contortions are asked for. A healthy, normal way of moving is the best prerequisite for learning how to ride well. The reverse conclusion is valid as well: good riding helps to train healthy and natural movement. This is a very important understanding in today's movement-deficient world, where a deficiency of human exercise is the order of the day.

I do not want to write about a new system of riding in this book. On the contrary – the valid system of riding is examined from a different view-point. Therefore, excursions into the development of movement and the human anatomy will follow. Anyone who would like to become a better rider needs to know and understand their own body before being able to control it. Herein lies the key to the rider's feel. No book can replace a good education by a good instructor. Good education does not free riders of the obligation to self-train their own physical sensitivity and to try for better control over their own body. The aim of this book is to combine traditional teaching with physiological knowledge.

1.

Study of Movement and Riding

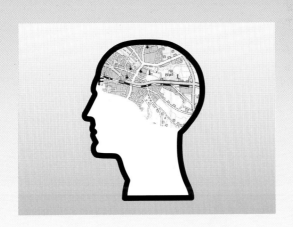

1.

How Children, Adolescents and Adults Learn about Movement

'Life is movement!' In our movement-deficient time we should always keep this phrase of a well-known therapist in mind. But how do we define movement, how is it created, how is it learned and applied?

Behavioural movement is something totally individual. Each human being moves differently, has his or her very own typical movements. These depend on build, constitution and the entire personality of each respective individual. Movement is governed by the human brain. Patterns of movement – as for example walking, standing, sitting, and leaping – can be stored in the brain in a way that they are automatically available upon request. Until the moment of birth cells mature in the brain, which multiply through cell division over and over again. This cell division terminates with birth when the process of learning begins. Single cells are connected through synapsis. A net of pathways and conduits develops. Those nets contain the individual supply of movement patterns. With the beginning of puberty a hormone is released which makes the continuous knotting of cells impossible. This means that new pathways can no longer be developed. For this reason childhood is of such imprinting significance for all areas of our life. In order to give a clearer idea of this process, I will compare the brain with a city map.

At the moment of birth, many single houses exist in the brain, and road construction is about to begin. A whole network of communications develops. When going from A to B, for example, one immediately builds in the process a direct road, which is then always used for this connection. This way children learn spontaneously complex movement patterns. The adult first has to search in the town in his head to see if there is a direct road from A to B. If not, maybe he can get to B through C.

Consequently an adult develops a certain movement from already available movement elements and falls back upon familiar movements. He is no longer able to build new roads in his town. In addition he is dependent on the fact of how well his network of communications is developed and how well he knows his way around – for it happens that direct roads have been buried, or that one takes an unnecessary detour. This picture also explains why an adult cannot find the way the second time, although he executed this movement once before. An alternative way has to be established over deviations and must become well grooved in order to find bifurcations 'blindfolded'. Therefore an adult has to practise and train new movement patterns.

The conduction in the nerve pathways of the brain is incredibly fast. Thus, even the longer way around can be used almost without any loss of time. However, most participants of top-performance sports learned their discipline in early childhood, and the few top-ranking athletes who

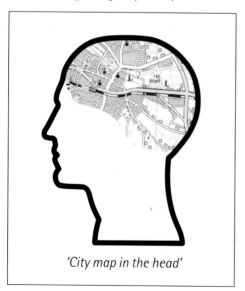

'City map in the head'

started later in life had the opportunity to collect many movement experiences during their childhood.

Unused roads in the brain are likely to become defective, buried and in need of repair. The less an adult trains his multitude of movements the more will be lost. This manifests itself in poor posture and an imbalance of all behavioural movement, our civilised ailment. To clear and revive buried pathways is a laborious and time-consuming job.

Please, do not close the book now and regard yourself as a hopeless case if you did not start riding in early childhood. Riding is a sport which is based upon a multitude of familiar movement patterns. For example, in therapeutic riding the walk of the horse is so valuable because the horse's back transfers the normal pattern to the trunk of the rider. Riding has much in common with walking. The movements and required reactions in the trunk are often nearly identical. This is one of the reasons for the significant health benefits of riding. Even as a latecomer the odds of becoming a good rider are very favourable!

Movement is the expression of the entire personality of an individual. The 'inner' person influences the quality of movement decisively. When feeling good, one's posture and movement will be very different from when feeling mentally low. An erect posture, a straight and free walk is always a sign of inner security and mental balance. A person who collapses not only hides the head between the shoulders but hides his entire personality from the world around.

Enemies of the ability to learn a movement are fear, stress, monotony, chaos, over-demand on strength and coordination. Fear blocks the ability to move. When afraid, a person evades into protective reflexes like clamping, pulling up the hands, flexing the trunk (in extreme

cases up to the foetal crouch position). Stress in contrast creates only automatisms. Under stress one can only act automatically, but an adequate fine tuning to the immediate situation is no longer possible. Thus, when riding under stress, one can no longer react to the acute demands of the moment, and for certain one cannot experiment with new movement experiences. For example, a stressed-out rider will execute a half-halt merely by rote, without being able to adjust to the subtle messages of the horse and the resulting necessary strength and timing of the aids.

Monotony, rigid routine, mulish repetition, pure boredom ultimately make progress impossible, because learning is inseparably connected with the desire for new experiences. The other extreme of chaos is equally unfruitful, as one can no longer distinguish between newness and familiarity. Successful learning takes place in small increments on a narrow edge between monotony and chaos.

When new subjects are added, the remaining fundamental requirements have to remain constant. On a new horse one will initially execute familiar exercises. A new movement is acquired in small steps with increasing degree of difficulty: for example, the halt is made at first in a certain section of the long side, then on a predetermined place on the track, and finally, without the help of a wall or fence, at X . . .

Over-demand of strength and coordination is mostly the result of setting the wrong goal. However, wrong goals are often not established by the instructor, but by the student himself.

Three basic principles are identifiable from the model of movement development during childhood:

■ from the trunk to the extremities
■ from the raw form to the fine form
■ through movement to posture

The trunk develops before the extremities since it needs to ensure their stability. At first the infant learns to support himself on the shoulder, then on the elbow, then on the hands, and when this is secure the fingers begin to grasp. Calculated movements of the extremities are only possible when the trunk is stable: from the trunk to the extremities.

Movements are initially large-scale and are executed with more effort than necessary. Gradually they are optimised and applied economically with the least possible effort: from the raw form to the fine form. It is possible to move in a new position before having obtained the necessary coordination. The infant will at first stagger and rock on all fours before being able to balance in this stance; walking will be possible before standing still: through movement to posture.

When learning how to ride we have to submit to the same basic principles. At first the trunk has to become stable before control of the extremities can be considered at all. To ask for quiet hands and heels down in the first lesson would be utter nonsense! From the trunk to the extremities. A person intending to work on the fine form immediately will face a goal too far removed. At first one has to be content with the raw form, then one can start working and polishing piece by piece: from the raw form to the fine form.

The subtle balance, the seemingly quiet seat is achieved initially through increased movement. The typical unstable seat of the beginner is not incorrect but the first step to finding balance during movement: through movement to posture.

The exact image of a movement can be helpful. In order to school one's own inner image of a movement, it is very important to watch good riders perform. A child can spontaneously copy a new movement just by watching it done. For example, they watch another child at the rising trot, and know then how to do it as well, without being shown or having explained to them any in-between steps. An adult requires both image of the movement and explanation. Adults learn much more consciously, have to give things a lot more thought. They demand many more details, explanations and learning steps; each new movement has to be structured and assembled. The image of the final and correct movement is important in order to be able to properly sort and compose the pieces of the puzzle.

A typical example is a beginner who is allowed off the lunge for the first time in order to cool down the horse. The adult will ask at once: how do I get the horse to move, what do I have to do, how do I steer ...? When then given a technical description it is bound to fail, since it cannot be sensitively adjusted to the horse, and frustration is inevitable. The student would fare much better by trying to experience the situation, to trust the horse's movement. This again is the domain of the children. They regard their school horse as a friend and trust him much more uninhibitedly. They are much more open to learn from the horse. So my wish for many riders is: remain a child to some degree, switch off the technically-thinking mind and open up uninhibitedly to new experiences.

The learning of a movement happens therefore not only in practical operation, but to a large degree in the head. In the science of sports this is called and utilised as *mental* training. Mental training consists of a systematic, repeated and conscious image of the execution of a movement with optimal inner feedback of the sequences and the result. This definition contains a load of information. A movement is precisely thought through and then again and again visualised by the inner eye. In the process the movement becomes optimised and one adapts positively to it. The sequence and the success of the movement and with it the meaning and practicality become clear. Once a rider understands the necessity of sitting upright, they will try harder to sit this way. Mental preparation is extremely important, especially in high-performance sports. Very quickly a rider can block themself internally or externally through stress, fear and performance pressure, so they do not produce their true ability.

1.2 The Training of the Rider

Nowhere else can we find so much insecurity, so many different opinions as when asking the question: what are the logical and consecutive steps in the training of a rider? What should be learned first, what second? What should we pay attention to? Should a beginner start out with or without stirrups, first in the half seat or in the full seat . . . There are surely many different answers to questions like these. Different opinions become evident in the placings of young rider tests. It is important to regard a student not as a composition of faults (head bobs, legs placed wrongly, hands turned wrongly . . .), but as a learner on his journey who masters some things before others.

In order for instruction to be successful, the instructor has to recognise the next step the student has to negotiate. In all other types of sport the training is broken down in precise and systematically arranged steps. Riding is a very complex sport and is afflicted with particular learning difficulties. Success depends not only on the rider but also on the environment and especially the horse. The process of learning how to ride cannot be forced into a general pattern. Questions like: 'How many hours will be necessary on the lunge?' or 'How many lessons to achieve a certain standard?' so often asked by parents or beginners are impossible to answer.

A riding school is not a driving school, where a minimum number of lessons is mandatory for the horse driver's licence, and where students try to outdo each other as to who required the least number of lessons. Circumstances and the horse play an important role. To be released from the lunge earlier is not necessarily an advantage. Students who work more extensively on the perfection of their seat on the lunge, often, later on, make greater progress, since they are not confronted with all demands at once. It is not for nothing that an institution like the celebrated Spanish Riding School, whose riders are famous for their masterly seat, demands months of basic training exclusively on the lunge.

On the other hand, riding off the lunge has a significant psychological effect and is highly motivating. To weigh one against the other is the demanding task of the instructor. Riding cannot be learned following a rigid system. And yet there are criteria concerning what has to be learned first, and what can be built upon later. The riding doctrine divides this into *seat, aids, feel* and *influence*. This is the road of training I would like to outline in the following pages, but in addition I have subdivided the various subjects. This course of training is comparable with the scales of training for the horse.

Contact

Contact with the horse is the most important basic requirement for making learning possible. A good inner direct line to the horse dismantles fear, and creates a situation of mutual trust. Often, such a connection with the horse is stronger than technical skill. Who does not know about the observation that horses who are known to jump to the side, for an unpleasant surprise, would never do this under a child? And the really great achievements are based on this inner contact, this mutual feeling between rider and horse.

Balance

The first goal demanded from the student on the horse is balance. Without balance you would fall off or would have to hold on with pure strength. The development of balance, especially for the upper body, is prerequisite for any future equestrian education.

Ride for once without a saddle in order to feel the horse's movements directly and to be forced to react accordingly. To be able to balance on the horse's back in each gait vertically and horizontally is the first goal of a beginner rider.

Suppleness

Once balance is achieved in a movement, we do not have to expend any more strength than necessary for a certain situation. No muscle is permanently in tension, but rather a rhythmic tightening and relaxing of the muscles develops parallel to the horse's movement. Suppleness is not to be confused with looseness or limpness of the muscles. Muscles work economically under the correct suppleness, optimally for one's own body, and the basic tension of the muscles is conformed to the situation at hand – in the collected trot stronger than at the walk on a long rein. Only a relaxed seat facilitates the control and independent movement of the extremities, the basis for finely tuned aids.

Secure Seat

A deep and secure seat is the prerequisite for effective influence. All of the muscles responsible for the erectness of the seat must possess a good basic tension without sacrificing suppleness. Part of the secret of riding is to be able to control the horse in this fashion with the seat. The rider then sits in the horse, not on the horse, horse and rider become one.

Parallel to the development of the seat is the learning of the application of the aids.

Dexterity

At first, the application of the aids is acquired purely technically; this is where the leg belongs, the hands are turned that way ... Certainly the aids will be very coarse at the beginning, and until the student is able to fine tune. A beginner will negotiate turns with a great deal more effort than a more advanced rider. The possibility of practising isolated aids is very limited. The rider is immediately challenged with a very complex task and often overtaxed. Therefore the instructor has to tailor the various situations of application to the abilities of the student.

Feel

The feel of the rider, the optimal communication between horse and rider, is to be regarded as the climax of all equestrian abilities. This feel is not the innate privilege of some few highly gifted talents but a major learning goal for any rider. The sensitive communication with the horse must be learned and taught from the very first lesson on. This is the only way the rider will eventually achieve the skill to apply aids harmoniously to the task at hand and at the same time to the reactions of the horse.

2.

Physiology of Movement

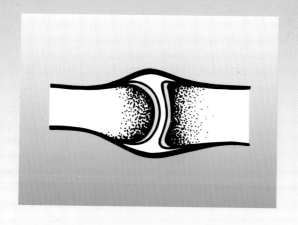

2.1 Joints: Structure, Function and Biomechanics

A *joint* is the moveable connection of two bones. Joints facilitate movement and, due to their structure, determine certain directions and dimensions of movement. This joint consists of a *ball* and a *socket*.

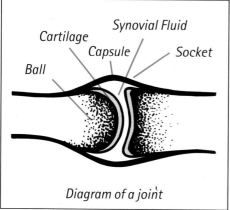

Cartilage
Synovial Fluid
Capsule
Socket
Ball

Diagram of a joint

The two facing joint surfaces are covered with a layer of articular cartilage, which protects the bones like a buffer. On the outside, the joint is encased by the *capsule*. The cavity of the joint is filled with a liquid which acts as a lubricant. In addition, this liquid contains nutrients for the cartilage since there is no blood circulation, so nutrition has to take place through diffusion. The joint capsule is surrounded by fine nerve tissue where receptors are located that report even the tiniest change in the joint regarding position of the joint and tension in the capsule. The musculature covers the joint as a moving element and attaches through the tendon to the periosteum. Sometimes a muscle connects directly with the joint capsule (shoulder), and this capsule is, as a result, even more sensitive to the most minute changes; cramped shoulders, for example, block the entire shoulder joint. Different movements can take place in joints depending on their type. A *hinged*

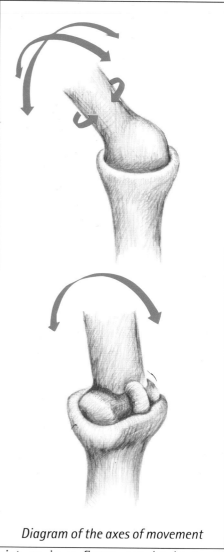

Diagram of the axes of movement

joint, as in a finger, can be bent and stretched. There exists only one dimension of movement. The joint of the hand is a different matter. There exist two dimensions of movement, it can be stretched and bent, and it can be turned, either in the direction of the thumb or the little finger. The rotating of this joint is a mixture of these two main directions of movement. It becomes even more complicated with a *ball and socket joint* like the shoulder or

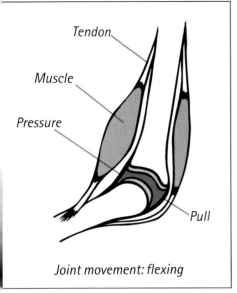

Tendon

Muscle

Pressure

Pull

Joint movement: flexing

the hip. There are three dimensions of movement which can be tied together: they are bending and stretching, abduction and adduction and rotating to the inside and outside.

If we would move only in those visualised dimensions our movements would appear jerky like a robot's. A beautiful and economical movement always combines all three dimensions and is fluid and round.

Consequently, a movement has to always be three dimensional – luckily no blue print has been developed yet for the fourth dimension!

What happens now during movement in the joint itself? As you can learn from the drawing, the one joint partner moves around the other one. Thus a pulling force is exerted onto the joint on one side and a pressure force on the other. The joint capsule is most relaxed in the middle position, and the joint experiences the least inner compression. The nerves record this as standard value. This position also facilitates diffusion. No nutrients can diffuse if the pressure within the joint is too high, which in the long run will damage the cartilage and thus the joint. For this reason the receptors of the joint capsule immediately signal deviations from the middle position, in order that the muscles will react automatically and restore the norm. This is also why the musculature is the most relaxed in the middle position of the joints.

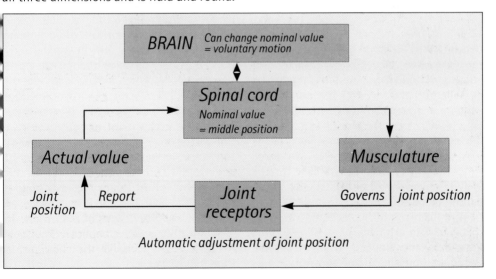

BRAIN *Can change nominal value = voluntary motion*

Spinal cord
Nominal value = middle position

Actual value

Musculature

Joint position | Report

Joint receptors

Governs | joint position

Automatic adjustment of joint position

Muscles: Structure, Function and Biomechanics

The *musculature* is our most important kinetic organ. Its structure conforms to the multitude and function of our movements. The whole muscle is divided into separate longish fibres, similar to an orange. Each single fibre possesses elastic and contractible elements which are able to shorten and stretch. Basically there are

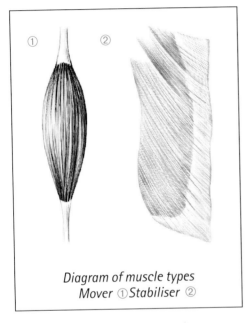

Diagram of muscle types
Mover ① Stabiliser ②

two different kinds of muscle fibres. First the *dynamic* fibres, responsible for movement, which can be contracted to a large degree, and secondly the *static* fibres which are responsible for posture. The big muscles of the arms and legs consist mostly of dynamic fibres, since most of the movement takes place there. The trunk which has to ensure the stability for the body to move, therefore possesses a larger portion of static fibres.

This has to be considered for the specific training of muscles. Here, I think mostly of the popular training of the abdominal muscles in the form of sit-ups

and jack knife. In this case the abdominal muscles have to cover distance. They are being trained for movement not posture. Only a small percentage of abdominal muscle fibres can be accessed this way. The hoped-for success often fails to be achieved, in spite of hard training!

Now, what happens in a muscle during a work out?

In order to better illustrate the three main methods of the working of a muscle,

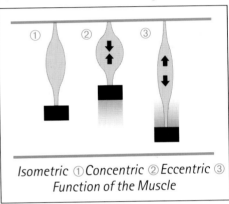

Isometric ① Concentric ② Eccentric ③
Function of the Muscle

I recommend that you pick up a heavy object and hold it in front of your body with the elbow at about a ninety degree angle. On this occasion the upper arm flexor has to perform holding duty. This is called an *isometric* contraction, the muscle works without negotiating a distance. If you flex the elbow further while holding the object, the upper arm flexor shortens, thus covering a distance, the muscle works *concentrically*. When slowly lowering the arm again it is still the flexor working (not the extender!), this time it lengthens during the effort. This *eccentric* contraction is the most difficult, causing muscle soreness very easily. It is the most important kind of muscular effort for the stabilisation of the joints. Please note, that it is not the shortening of a muscle that is the most important exercise, but the slow and controlled release against resistance (weight, gravity . . .). This is the best way to train a muscle.

A muscle is amply supplied with blood since it requires a lot of oxygen for its function. If a muscle is under constant tension circulation becomes impossible due to the increased pressure in the muscle. No new nutrients are delivered to the individual fibres. Once the stored supply of oxygen is used up the muscle can no longer function properly. In addition, lactic acid, the waste product of the metabolism in the muscle, can no longer be carried off. The acid leads to pain in the muscle which then contracts in a cramp-like fashion causing it to receive even less blood supply...a frequently occurring vicious cycle. On the other hand, if a muscle works rhythmically in intervals, and in interplay with its opponents, it can continually receive new oxygen and will not deposit lactic acid.

Please note that a muscle can only work meaningfully over a longer period of time when it is not under constant tension, but rather in a rhythmic interplay with other muscles.

The Interplay of Muscles

When moving a joint with calculation and direction, it is never a single muscle that is in action, but always a concentric muscle in combination with an interrelated eccentric muscle. When the extender works concentrically, in other words creates movement, the flexor checks the movement in an eccentrically yielding way, and the movement can thus be executed with utmost precision. In a well performed movement the joint is therefore guided and secured from all sides!

Movement usually does not take place in a single joint – it starts and continues throughout the whole body through so called *muscle chains*. You can easily duplicate this by letting both arms hang alongside the body and then starting to turn the thumbs forward and outward. The

movement continues, the palms face outside, the shoulders are brought back, the thorax becomes erect and the head comes up. This is called an *extension pattern*. If you turn the hands into the opposite direction, shoulders, back and head become round, and a *flexion pattern* emerges. This is an interesting observation when transferred to riding regarding the hand position. How much more difficult it is for somebody to sit upright with the

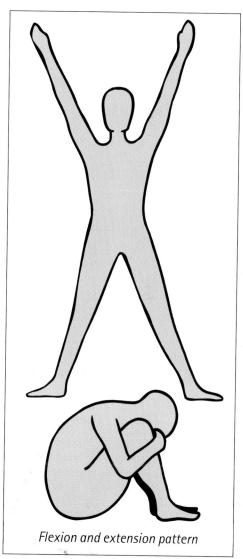

Flexion and extension pattern

hands in a turned down position, since two counteracting muscle chains are activated!

Most of our movements happen subconsciously. The innervation of a muscle happens due to certain reflexes. The musculature is in a constant basic tension, called *tone*, which, for example is lower when lying down than when standing up. The change from this basic tension adjusts to a situation without us thinking about it. Thus joint position and posture determine a large part of our way of moving. A muscle can only react and operate optimally when this basic tension is conforming to a certain situation.

This chapter already illustrates why the sport of riding is so exceptional. When sitting on a horse, most joints can be found in their physiological middle position. The musculature is not exposed to endurance stress, but rather a highly coordinated interplay of all muscles is required. In compliance with the situation, the trunk acts as a stabiliser as the extremities move to provide subtle influence on the horse.

In physiotherapy, the smallest deviations from the middle position of a joint are important to recognise for the therapeutic treatment they give. They are more important than extensive stretching and large movements. Strengthening and training devices recede more and more and give way to coordination and agility training. To that end, it is necessary to know better and understand our own bodies, so we are able to use them economically in everyday life as well as in sports – the key to many a success.

3.

Pelvis – Centre of Movement

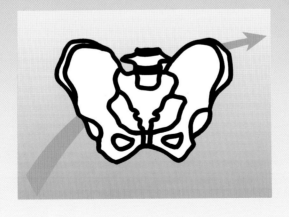

Basic Anatomy

The pelvis is the control centre of our movements. Therefore it is important to know some basic anatomy in order to be able to develop a feel for the position and the mobility of the pelvis. From a purely anatomical point of view the pelvis is a bony ring which consists of three major parts: the two large wings (called *ilia*)

and the *sacrum* which joins with the rear of the wings thus creating a solid ring.

From a functional or rather kinetic point of view, the *hip joint* and the *lumbar spine* are part of the pelvis. Each movement of the pelvis necessitates movement in these joints.

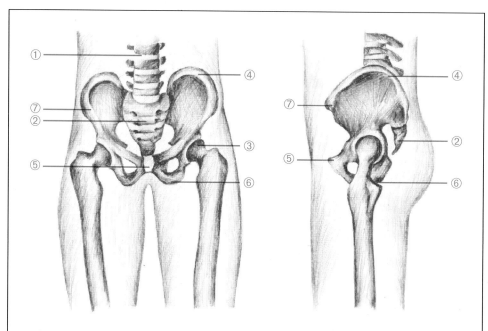

① *Lumbar spine*

② *Sacrum*

③ *hip joint*

④ *Iliac crest*

⑤ *Pubic bone*

⑥ *Ischial tuberosities (Seat bones)*

⑦ *Anterior superior iliac spine (A.S.I.S.)*

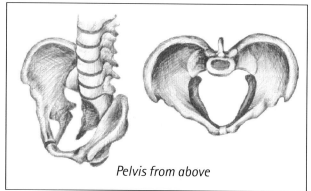

Pelvis from above

Pelvis with hip and lumbar spine from the front and side

3.2 Body Proportions and Individual Constitution

The pelvis divides the length of the body into two halves. Of course these two halves are not always of the same size. From it one can draw important conclusions for balance.

A person with a short upper body and long legs will find it easier to balance on the back of a horse than somebody with a longer upper body. These differences become especially apparent during the growth spurts of children and adolescents. When sitting, two children may seem of the same height, but when standing their height may differ by a full head. These differences become clear when examining the growth development from child to adult.

The build of a child is characterised by a large head and a long trunk; in relation the arms and legs are short. Growth takes place in spurts, at one time the trunk is involved, at another time the extremities. As a result young people often appear inharmonious, sometimes lanky, and then again stocky, until the proportions eventually even out. Then the legs should be of the same length as the trunk and head. If the trunk remains the longer lever,

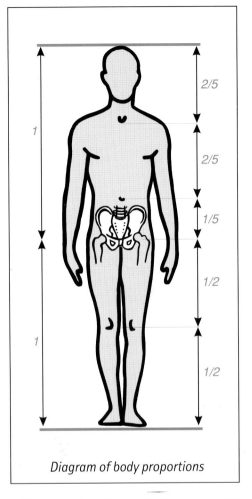

Diagram of body proportions

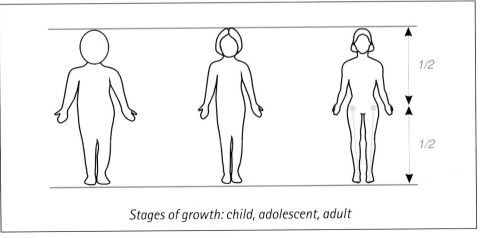

Stages of growth: child, adolescent, adult

we speak of a 'seat giant', and if the legs are longer one will not notice this until the individual rises from a sitting position and unfolds his full height. In order to estimate the body proportions correctly it is important to draw the imaginary line truly at the height of the hip joints and not at the waist! A long pelvis can often feign long legs, but in relation to the hip joints the upper body is the longer lever after all.

Differences in the width of the pelvis play only a minor role in riding. The main difference of the pelvis between a man and woman is mostly the width of the iliac crest or hip bone, the actual seat basis of the pelvic branches shows very minor distinctions. A good fit of the saddle is important for the width of the pelvis, in order to be able to distribute the weight as evenly as possible over the branches of the pelvis (or *ramus of ischium*). For a comfortable seat, the width and shape of

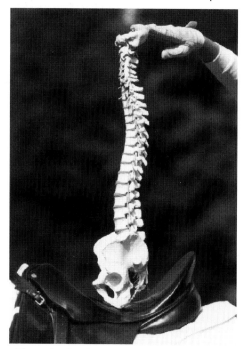

The spinal column and pelvis on top of a saddle

the horse's back is much more critica Anatomical advantages for riding ar obviously not derived from a 'smal difference'. Men as well as women rid with great success and there is no ridin instruction where aids for men and wome are prescribed differently, unless th woman rides side saddle! There is not onl no specific sex-related riding instruction there are also no sex-related advantage for men or women in the sport. From performance point of view, men an women appear to have absolutely equa rights in all three classical disciplines dressage, jumping and eventing. This is no always the case in other sports.

3.3 Palpating the Most Important Landmarks on Your Own Body

When learning to ride it is of little use to know simply the rigid anatomy. In order to understand fully this chapter about anatomy with life, it would be helpful fo you to get a stool, shorts, a music stand fo the book (so you can have both hands free and sit in front of a mirror. When you support both hands at your waist you rest on the *iliac crest*. Before feeling further, a few important terms have to be explained. Some words have a different meaning in everyday language and anatomy. In common language a backache can mean shoulders, loin or even lower down. Anatomy is much more specific. One speaks, for instance, of the *small of the back* which is the bony processes of the lumbar spine. Another popular and frequently used term is *hip*. We think in general of the iliac crest (the hip bone), the hip joint and the upper part of the thigh. In this book, the word hip relates solely to the hip joint, since this is where the movement takes place. Once again please palpate the *iliac crest* by supporting both hands at the waist and follow with your index finger

The pointed, anterior hip bone – the anterior superior iliac spine or A.S.I.S.

along the ridge to the front until you reach a sharp corner. Here the bone is usually very close under the skin and this area is especially sensitive to being bumped. This corner is very important for the observation and palpability of the position of the pelvis and is called *A.S.I.S.* (anterior superior iliac spine).

With the hands at the waist the thumbs can palpate a similar corner toward the rear. A dimple in the skin is visible on many people at this place of the sacrum. Between these two rearmost *A.S.I.S.* the *sacrum* joins with the ring of the pelvis. One can follow the sacrum all the way down to the *coccyx*; when sitting the *sacrum* itself does not carry any weight.

In the classical riding theory one can find this fundamental phrase: 'The rider sits on the two seat bones and on the crotch'. The two *seat bones* can be found easily or not

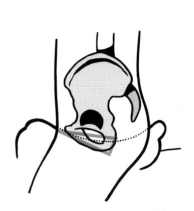

Base of the seat from the side

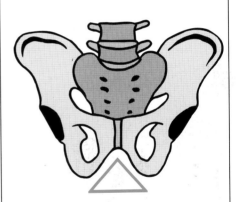

Base of the seat from the front

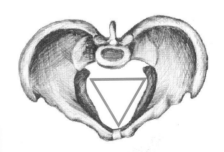

Base of the seat from above

depending on the firmness of the stool and one's own individual padding. To locate the crotch is more difficult. This is meant to be the *branch of the pubic bone*, but the lowest part, not the upper one!

The *pubic bone* can be easily palpated by sliding the fingers from the belly downward until one meets a bony resistance. There one can feel the upper edge; the *pubic bone* proceeds from there obliquely down and back. At the lower edge it divides into two branches, which lead to the *ischial tuberosities* or seat bones. Thus an actual seat base with a triangular shape is created, which should be loaded evenly when sitting upright correctly. A three-point support is always especially stable – a three-legged stool hardly ever tips over in contrast to its four-legged relatives. The number three appears again and again in the entire human organism. Optimal three-point loading of the feet (heels, little toe- and large toe base), the construction of the individual

vertebrae, the three dimensional movement . . .

Functionally, the *hip joints* and lumbar spine (*LS*) are part of the pelvis. The lumbar spine is easily palpable by its *spinous processes*. They are especially distinct when rounding the back, and recess more and more as the back is hollowed.

The localisation of the *hip joint* is not so easy. Most people follow the request to support the hands on the hip by putting them into the waist, but there they contact the iliac crest, as experienced before.

The easiest way to palpate the *hip* is while standing. One can feel the *hip bones* laterally at the height of the *hip joints*. This is where the widest part of the pelvis is. When turning the whole leg to the inside or outside, one can feel the forward- and backward movement of the hip bones. The *hip joint* is located about half way between the hip bone and the pubic bone. There one

Localisation of the hip joint from the side   *Pelvis from the front*

can feel the pulse of the leg artery, which can be found exactly above the hip joint.

When looking closely at the drawing once more you can see that the *hip joint* is located higher than the base of the seat. This means that the hip is not loaded when sitting but is free and can be suspended in relaxation!

Most of the pelvic muscles are part of the hip musculature which I will discuss in greater depth in the leg chapter. For the proper position of the pelvis, it is important to open the legs and let them hang far enough so that the pelvis can contact the saddle as deeply as possible.

The large *buttock muscles* (bottom cheeks) can even lift the seat bones a small distance. This can be easily experienced on a stool. The feel of sinking deeper after releasing the muscle is important. The so-called *adductors* can lift the pelvis from the low position as well. Their insertion is easily felt at the pubic bone where a firm cord of tendons is present. In reality these *adductors* originate all along the branch of the pubic bone and reach all the way to the seat bone. When these tense or, in other words, become shorter and thus thicker one then sits on the adductors instead of on the seat bones.

Unfortunately, it is difficult to tense or rather relax muscles as desired when riding. Therefore it is important to practise the control of this musculature in many other situations. Often this is not so easy since many muscle groups work involuntarily, that is to say fully automatically. They are not necessarily subject to our consciousness and we are not necessarily conscious of their tension and relaxation. An important example is the musculature of the pelvic floor. It tenses the floor of the pelvic ring and carries the inner organs. It is not responsible for any joint movement, and yet it is of utmost importance for riding. You surely have experienced how

impossible it is to sit supply when having to go to the bathroom urgently. But the pelvic floor can tense for many other reasons such as fear, stress, insecurity...This musculature reacts very sensitively to inner moods and ups and downs. We cannot discuss the musculature of the pelvic floor with every riding instructor. It is important to know that it takes inner-balance and relaxation to open the floor of the pelvis.

The last important muscle group is the *abdominal musculature*. A tight band runs from the A.S.I.S. to the pubic bone. Below it are muscles, nerves and vessels. The abdominal muscles insert on the pubic bone in a straight band in the middle and two diagonal cords, at the band between the pubic bone and the A.S.I.S. at the inside of the pelvic wings and continue to the thorax and attach to the ribs. One can best palpate the most important lower insertions by lying flat on one's back, the lumbar spine pressed hard against the floor, and by angling the legs so hips and knees are at a right angle. Your hands are then able to feel the contractions of these muscles at these insertions. In the following chapters I will discuss in depth their role for riding.

3.4 The Ideal Position of the Pelvis on the Horse

The Dressage Seat

Elegant and effortless, full of harmony and calmness, this is what a good dressage seat should look like. Even the Greek general Xenophon describes in his riding theory, passed on from antiquity, that the seat has nothing in common with sitting on a chair, but rather resembles standing upright with slightly straddled and bent legs. This comparison is extremely important when

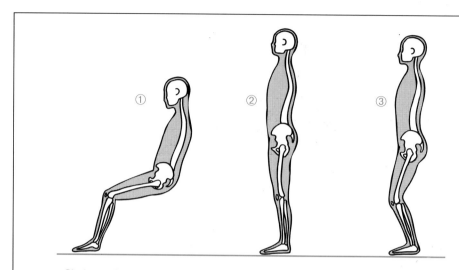

Sitting 1 Standing 2 Standing with slightly flexed and straddled legs 3

examining the position of the pelvis more closely. The A.S.I.S. in the front are in the same line as the pubic bone. We can imagine a vertical line which touches both points. It is in this middle position of the pelvis that the base of the seat can establish the best contact with the saddle. Also each movement originating from below can be optimally absorbed and cushioned from a middle position of a joint.

The lumbar spine must retain its natural slight hollowness; if it were straightened,

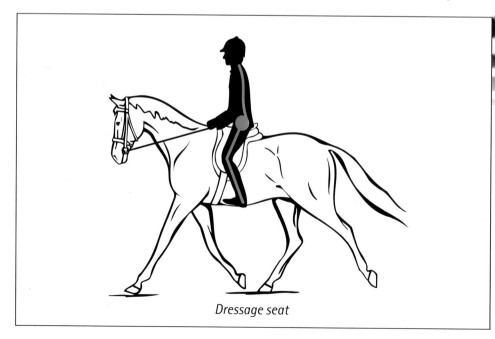

Dressage seat

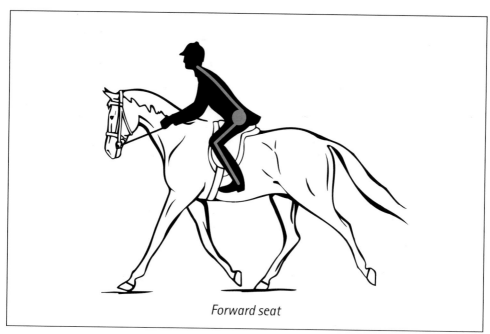

Forward seat

the rider would be stiff as a stick. The most important criterion for the hip is total relaxation. Watch as many riders as possible and try to see the difference: who really swings supply in the hip (localisation!) and who wobbles loosely in the waist with locked hips?

The dressage rider should be deeply rooted in the horse. Movements and shifting of weight should be invisible to the onlooker.

The Forward Seat

The transition from the dressage seat to the *forward seat* should be soft and fluid. There is no rigid standard, no measurement, as to the angle the hip should be flexed. This depends at all times on the circumstances, the horse and the situation. The forward seat includes the whole range from the fairly close half seat to the extreme release over a jump.

The actual position of the pelvis does not change. The A.S.I.S. are still aligned with the pubic bone, only this line is no longer vertical. The hip joint creates the centre of rotation, not the lumbar spine! Since the hip joint is located higher than the seat bones, they are automatically pushed a little to the rear, owing to the forward bending from the hip, and the rider can thus balance himself over his thighs and knees. This is facilitated by the shorter stirrup and the resulting increased angulation of the knee.

3.5 Unmounted Exercises: The Pelvis

You had best sit down in front of a mirror and put your index fingers on the *A.S.I.S.* In the following movement of the pelvis you are basically rolling over the two (pelvic) branches of the seat triangle.

When rolling forward, the *A.S.I.S.* come closer to the thighs, the hip joints close and the seat bones point to the rear. The lumbar spine is stretched and disappears finally in the hollow of the back. When you roll the pelvis over the seat bones to the rear, the *A.S.I.S.* move away from the thighs, and the seat bones point forward. Thus the back becomes round and one can palpate the spinous processes from the lumbar vertebrae. Now just sit comfortably down on your hands. Close your eyes and imagine a riding lesson. You hear the instructor saying loudly: 'Sit up straight . . .' (I will leave the more pictorial embellishments up to my readers).

At once a jolt runs through your body, zap – and you sit up. Do you? What do you feel with your hands? When erecting the body so abruptly, in nine out of ten cases the seat bones will be pushed energetically to the rear, but generally one would like to ride forward! The first goal when sitting on a horse is to find the middle position of the pelvis as the *basis of the seat*; this position enables us to follow securely all movements of the horse. There are three criteria how you can find this middle position for yourself:

1. Roll several times over the seat bones as explained above and try to find the position where you can feel the highest point of the seat bones. Under no circumstances can they point forward, but they may rather show a little tilt to the rear.

2. Palpate the A.S.I.S. and the pubic bone and try to line up these points vertically.

3. With one hand, palpate the spinous processes of the lumbar spine. Execute the rearward and forward movement of the pelvis as explained above several times. When the pelvis rolls back you can clearly feel the spinous processes. When rolling the pelvis forward they disappear in a hollow, and when rolling the pelvis strongly to the front two muscle cords on the right and left of the spine become tight like ropes (active hollow back). In the middle position of the pelvis the spinous processes have just disappeared, but the back muscles are still relaxed.

It is important to understand that a natural 'hollow back' is normal when sitting! If we moved the pelvis so far back that the lumbar spine was totally straight, the back could no longer swing with the movement. On the one hand, it surely

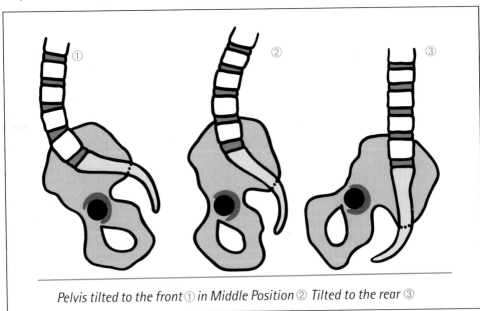

Pelvis tilted to the front ① in Middle Position ② Tilted to the rear ③

makes sense that an S-shaped spine can cushion movement better; on the other hand, the last lumbar vertebra – called L 5 – is so limited in its mobility that it is at the end of its range when the lumbar spine is 'straight', and it gets jammed there. This is a frequent cause for lower back pain, especially after sitting for a long time. Now, sit down over a corner of the stool and position your feet to the rear, for this arrangement of the thighs corresponds more closely to the riding seat. Now recall the image of the seat triangle again and try in your mind to tilt this three-legged chair. This would correspond to the shifting of the weight when riding and this is the meaning of expressions like: 'Load the inside, inner hip forward and down-ward ...' The actual movement is tiny when sitting as quietly as possible.

Now, try consciously to tense the large buttock muscle one more time and to sink down onto the seat bone when relaxing it. Or palpate the insertions of the adductor, press the legs together and relax them again. When either one of these two muscle groups is firmly tightened, it is very difficult to execute the pelvic movement to the front or rear. This is comparable to the effort of breathing freely while tightly clenching the teeth.

3.6 Balancing the Pelvis with the Movement of the Horse

So, now it becomes interesting. You are best seated on a horse, at the same time holding the book in front of your eyes and riding alongside a hopefully available mirror, and please, nicely supple and relaxed, smiling and with utmost concentration . . .

The primary aim of this book is to convert theory into practice, but this does not make it any easier. It is best if you read this paragraph in quiet and then try the most understandable pointers in your next riding lesson. Of course it would be advantageous if this could be done on the lunge in order to fully concentrate on your seat. Otherwise the warming-up phase on a longer rein offers a welcome opportunity to direct the concentration towards our own balance – most horses will be very grateful for this. A rider with an unbalanced seat resembles a poorly packed and loosely fastened backpack. The better the weight is distributed in a backpack, the quieter it lies on the back, the less strenuous it is to walk; the weight of the backpack is then of secondary consid-eration. This applies to riding as well. Even a large and strong rider can appear lighter to a horse than a wobbly 'feather weight'. We should always keep in mind that the

Pelvis tilted to the front

in Middle Position

Tilted to the rear

rider upsets the natural balance of the horse. Another important aspect: the stiller the seat, the more the horse will be able to feel any changes in the seat.

Enough theory – you are mounted in the meantime and your horse is walking with calm and ground-covering steps through the arena. To begin, direct your concentration towards the points of contact with the saddle, in other words the two seat bones and the crotch. On a well-fitting saddle the upper rim of the pubic bone can support itself additionally on the pommel of the saddle. In order to find really deep contact and to become one with the movement of the horse, you can imagine unbuckling your legs and strapping on the four legs of the horse instead. Being moved, not moving actively, this is the motto!

The Walk

At the walk you can feel how the horse steps underneath. The walk of the horse transmits a movement similar to the human walk to the back of the rider – the walking pattern. The discovery of this fact explains the many astounding therapeutic effects of riding. At the walk the horse can transmit the walking pattern to a human unable to walk himself.

When concentrating on your own seat bones you can feel how they are moved forward by the horse when the corresponding hind foot leaves the ground. It feels as if you could walk on your seat bones. At the walk you can frequently see a rider mistakenly pushing, which manifests itself in a swinging, sometimes jerky movement of pelvis and upper body. Remember the comparison with the backpack – save your horse's back.

The Trot

At the trot the horse's back rises and falls

more evenly. Now imagine that your seat bones are a massaging hand. During a good massage the hand remains constantly on the body, it never loses contact, even when pressure and intensity change. The seat bones load the horse's back muscles laterally. The swinging back of a horse thus basically obtains its massage itself.

The Canter

For the canter, imagine again that your seat bones are your legs and that you are executing a small skip forward. In the process your inner hip advances automatically and is weighted more than the other, just as the riding theory demands.

This picture is often helpful when one is in the habit of lifting the seat off the saddle when cantering on. It is again important that we do not execute the skip but feel how the horse moves your pelvis into a kind of skip. Only when you have thus become a part of the movement can you try to influence it through emphasising, delaying or intensifying certain moments.

As soon as the pelvis loses its balance, either the upper body loses its quietness and/or the rider must cling tighter with the legs. The pelvis can be best balanced from the middle position, which you felt already on the stool, unmounted.

A well-known therapist once said during a training session for gait analysis: 'There is no correct position of the pelvis, the pelvis is always potentially mobile!' But the pelvis is only moveable when in its middle position, not when it has already arrived at either limit.

In order to find one's individual middle position during movement, the following exercise may be helpful.

Sitting in a regular middle position you bend your upper body (from the hip!)

forward, with the A.S.I.S. in front of the pubic bone. Automatically the seat bones carry less weight, and you sit no longer on the basis of the seat, but on the inner side of the thighs which are slightly tensed in the process (*fork seat*).

When leaning the upper body and pelvis backward, you can feel a tension at the front of the thighs. The knees want to slide up in a reflex-like movement and the lower rim of the pubic bone loses contact with the saddle (*chair seat*). The individual middle position is exactly the point where the legs can hang optimally from the hips and where neither an upward tension of the knee nor any weight on the inside of the thighs can be felt.

Remember again on this occasion, that the hip joint is located higher than the seat bones and that it is not carrying any weight when sitting.

The *adductors* represent the main problem

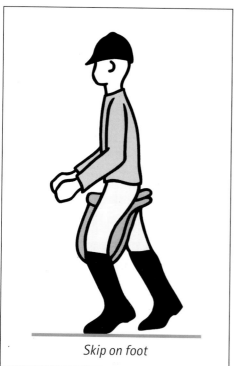

Skip on foot

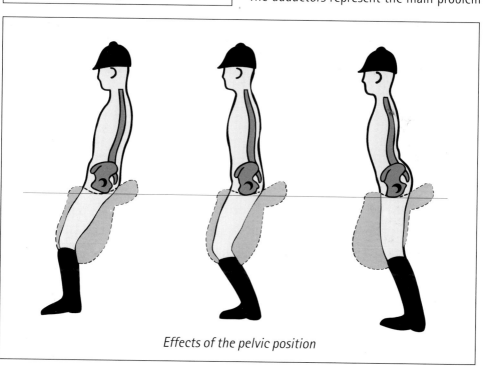

Effects of the pelvic position

for controlling the pelvis when riding, they often tense involuntarily – and at once the beautiful and deep seat is over with. Situations such as fear, excitement . . . initiate involuntarily a whole row of muscles, some of which are the adductors. This fact explains the often made observation that timid riders lose their balance more quickly. Also, a broad horse can overtax its rider; poorly extendable muscles are likely to react with tension to the stretching stimulus.

It is comforting to know that quiet and even pressure helps a tense muscle to relax. Therefore sit quietly, and often this problem will lessen during a session.

However, if the seat becomes unbalanced frequently, the muscles are repeatedly annoyed with new stimuli and become tighter.

Be brave. It takes a lot of courage to fully relax the muscles of the pelvis. Dare to relax the pelvis, commit it to the movement of the horse; only in this way will you be able to fully experience harmony with the horse.

4.

Centre of Stabilisation
Upper Body and Head

4.

Anatomy

The *spinal column*, the back bone of the trunk, is of utmost importance for our entire way of moving, for posture and movement. It consists of a row of single vertebrae and is therefore capable of manifold movement.

Each vertebra has two transverse processes and, at the rear, the palpable spinous process. The characteristic S-shape is ideal for cushioning shocks. If the spine was a straight rod, all shocks from below would arrive directly at the joints of the head, and the resulting headaches are easy to imagine.

The spinal column is divided into three sections, the *lumbar spine* (LS), the *thoracic spine* (TS) and the *cervical spine* (CS). When viewed from the side, we recognise that the three sections differ from each other mainly in the shape. CS and LS are curved to the front, TS to the rear. This is called CS/LS *lordosis* and TS *kyphosis*. In the TS area the *ribs* attach at the rear to the vertebrae, and continue from there to the *sternum*, thus creating the *thoracic cavity* or chest. The head could be called the last link of the vertebral chain, and it balances like a ball on top of a flexible and moving staff.

The musculature of the upper body is mainly responsible for the stabilisation of the trunk. Therefore it performs mostly

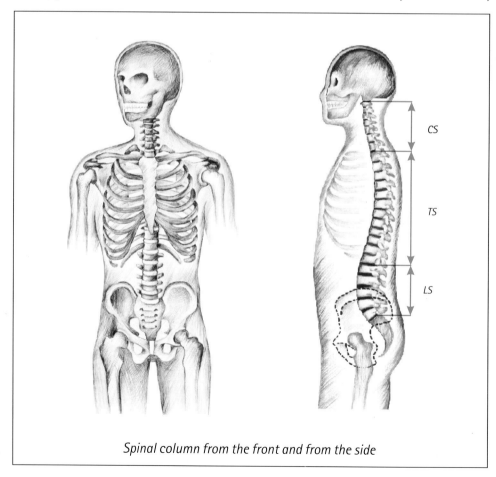

Spinal column from the front and from the side

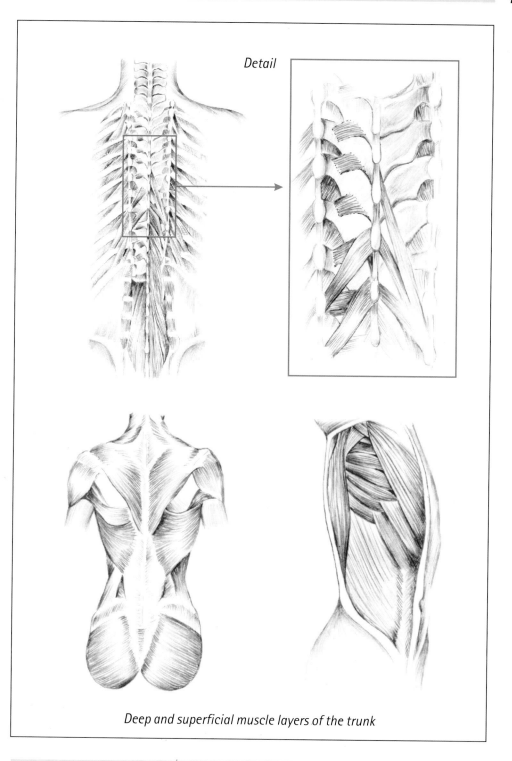

Detail

Deep and superficial muscle layers of the trunk

supporting duties, no major movements. As explained in the chapter about the physiology of the musculature, a major part of the trunk muscles consist of static muscle fibres.

The musculature of the trunk is laid down in individual layers as flat muscles. Unlike on the arm, there is no muscle with a large belly which attaches with two sinewy ends. The musculature of the trunk is like a plate and the muscle fibres are streaked with tiny tendons in order for the muscle to better withstand tractive stress. The deep layers consist of short muscles. For example, at the spine these short muscles reach only from one vertebra to the next, the surface layers stretch across the entire trunk like a net. On the back, this net reaches from the back of the head all the way down to the pelvis. The *deep, short muscles* govern the *fine motor skills* of the trunk, the *large surface muscles* facilitate *posture* and are the connection to the muscle chains of the extremities.

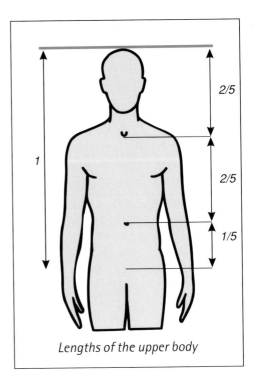

Lengths of the upper body

The trunk muscles are hardly subjected to the *voluntary motor skills*, especially the deep layer, so important for the fine motor skills. They react automatically, and can not be consciously controlled. They depend on the position of the joints, posture, your respective situation and the basic muscle tone.

4.2 Body Proportions and Individual Build

There exist certain approximate proportions for the upper body, just as the pelvis should ideally divide the body into two equally long halves. Let us think of the upper body as a tower, which consists of the three building blocks – pelvis, thorax and head. When intending to measure the separate lengths and to compare them with each other, one measures the pelvis

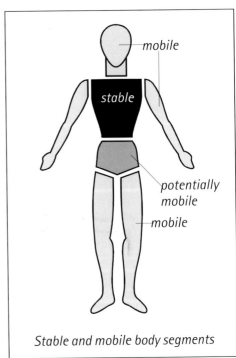

Stable and mobile body segments

from the height of the hip joints to the navel, the thorax from the navel to the hollow between the two collar bones and the head from this hollow to the top of the head. These 'norm values' would be $^1/_5$: $^2/_5$: $^2/_5$.

The division of the body into five *functional body segments* has proved very helpful for standardising the observation of movement. Arms, legs and head have only one contact surface with the adjoining body segments. Therefore they are very mobile and intended for movement. The pelvis adjoins two body segments and has the job of 'restraining' the movements of the legs (when riding, the movements of the back of the horse) and transmitting them to the spine in a coordinated fashion. For that purpose it continuously executes fine balancing acts in the hip joints and the LS. Three of the remaining four body segments adjoin the thorax. It therefore makes sense that the TS is intended to be the stabilising centre of posture and movement. It is a so-called dynamic stabilisation, since our chest moves continuously due to the breathing motion of the ribs, and it must react to movement.

Each segment of the upper body is moveable in all directions, but has one preferred direction of movement. Thus the building-block pelvis, which includes the LS, is assigned flexion and extension as the main functional movement, the thorax with the TS turning to the right and left. The head is the most freely moveable part – it can compensate in all directions. Every time the spine is bent sideways, it entails a very small turning movement due to the anatomy of the individual vertebrae. These so called weak points of the spine are mostly located at the transitions of the individual segments, since the directional change of movement takes place there. The individual lengths of the segments

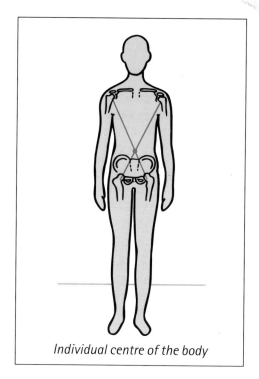

Individual centre of the body

play an important part in this connection. For example, a long pelvis would be a long lever and the transition to the thorax is located fairly high. Those people frequently have problems stabilising their upper body, and not only when riding.

Aside from the length, the width of the upper body plays an important part as well. The rule is that the distance between the shoulder joints should be twice as long as the distance between the hip joints. This is important for the balance when standing still and the shifting of weight when walking.

When drawing diagonal lines from the shoulder joints to the hip joints, they cross in the so called individual centre of the body. This is where the centre of movement is located, the middle posture. The musculature of the trunk and also of the extremities is mostly laid out along these imagined diagonals. Diagonal movements are economical for the body. For example, when walking the arms swing diagonally. Look at photos of any top athlete: again and again you will be able to observe diagonal twisting of the body. Only in this way is the body able to unfold its entire strength. When riding, the diagonal bracing of the body is of critical importance as well. It is not so obvious, but as soon as you begin riding through a corner, the inner hip and outside shoulder have to brace diagonally against each other. Otherwise one either collapses in the hip, or the shoulder stays behind the movement.

In order to illustrate the importance of the body width in relation to the way of moving, we can imagine the upper body as a triangle. A person with a broad pelvis and narrow shoulders has a low centre of

shift weight, a much longer distance has to be covered. When riding, this body type will have it easier with general balance but when riding through turns, and for influence, the upper body has to exert a greater effort compared to the unstable type. The latter type will not find it as easy to achieve balance during movement. However, a shifting of the weight can frequently be accomplished by merely thinking of it.

In the chapter about physiology I described basic facts about the basic tension of the musculature and explained that this basic tension, the tone, is dependent on situation. Thus, when lying down the tone is less than when standing. This is also the case for the above mentioned types of the upper body. The stable type will show less basic tone, and therefore the musculature

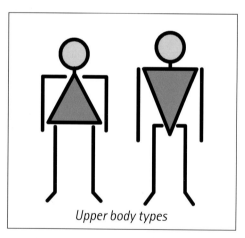

Upper body types

gravity, and when combined with a short and straight upper body, will have very good stability and the balance will not be easily upset. On the other hand, when the pelvis is narrower and the shoulders broader, it will certainly be more difficult to achieve and maintain balance. In this case the centre of gravity is higher, the seat more unstable. However, it will be easier to shift the weight. It is much harder for an upper body with a broad base to

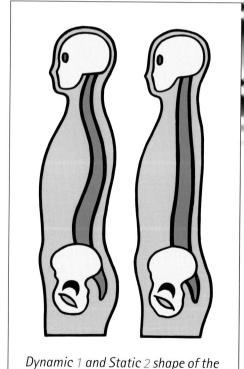

Dynamic 1 and Static 2 shape of the spinal column

will not be able to react as quickly. On the other hand we will find a higher basic tone with the unstable type and thus a higher reaction ability of the musculature.

Another important observation for the assessment of the type of movement is the shape of the upper body, when viewed from the side. In general a spine with increased oscillation can be ascribed to the *dynamic movement type*, a straight and flat back to the *stable posture type*.

The head represents a relatively heavy weight and is of critical significance for the entire balance. No matter what type of spine, when sitting, the head should always be above the pelvis, when standing, always above the feet; otherwise their balance cannot be right, and how would it then be possible to achieve balance with the movement of the horse?!

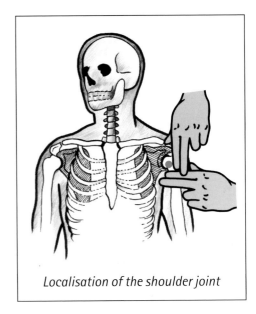

Localisation of the shoulder joint

4.3 Palpating the Most Important Landmarks on the Body

After so much theory it is your turn again. It is best if you stand in front of a mirror, or have two of you observe each other. What is the relation of the upper body to the legs, and how are the individual building blocks of the upper body arranged? Compare these with the drawing for this purpose.

In order to define the individual building blocks, first palpate the height of the hip joints as explained in the chapter about the pelvis. Further landmarks are the navel, the groove between the collar bones and the top of the head.

After having compared the different lengths, palpate the hip joints again, preferably right at the point where you can feel the pulse of the leg artery. Compare this distance to the distance between the shoulder joints. The centre of the shoulder joint can be found in the continuation of

the armpit fold, about two fingers width distance from above and from the side.

Now look at yourself from the side, how well are the oscillations of your spine defined? Do you tend toward the dynamic type, or rather the static one?

And how well do you know your back and posture so far? Do you know the weak points or problem angles? If yes, then please check if the transitions of the individual body segments are located there, or if your constitution features less advantageous levers. And try to judge for yourself, for example, the basic tone of your entire musculature – is it rather high and quick to react, or too high and thus tight/stiff. Do you carry your body slackly and therefore have a low basic tone which first needs to be initiated . . .?

It is certainly not easy to answer these questions by yourself when you know your own body so well, and in addition we do not always care to be honest with ourselves. Besides, the tone is extremely dependent on the time of day, mood, situation . . . Everybody possesses their own individual daily form, and you certainly know the time(s) of day when you

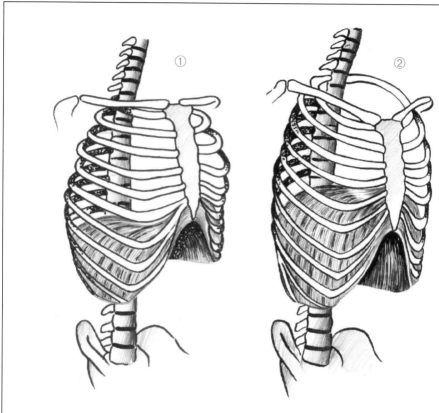

Thoracic cavity (chest) with diaphragm (inhaled 1 and exhaled 2)

feel especially fit for riding.

Further important landmarks of the upper body which you should know and palpate are the *sternum* and the lower arch of the ribs. The sternum is a flat and longish plate, and the ribs attach to its sides. The sternum should be vertical. If its lower part is pulled to the inside, a so-called *funnel chest*, it causes difficulties with breathing and posture.

Now palpate the *hollow between the collar bones* and the *lower tip of the sternum*. These two points should be on a vertical line to each other. The sternum tapers off toward its lower end. There the lower ribs connect as cartilage in an arc at an angle of about forty-five degrees. The

diaphragm, which is basically responsible for breathing, attaches to this arc. You can imagine that the chest as a cavity receives its stability by filling with air. This happens automatically when holding your breath, thus increasing the pressure in the chest, in order to achieve more stability and strength. When inhaling, the diaphragm lowers and the abdomen arches slightly to the front. If you put one hand on the rib arc and the other on the abdomen you can feel the breathing motion. Also, try to hold your breath under pressure – you can feel that everything becomes tight where your hands are.

The transition from the thorax to the neck/head can be felt at the hollow between the collar bones. In the back you can usually find a clearly protruding *spinous process*. This is usually the last cervical vertebra. When you feel with several fingers for the adjoining processes while tilting the head backwards, this one remains stationary and does not follow the direction of movement. Now slide upward with your fingers until you reach the *back of the head*. From there feel along to both sides, and you will find a thickening of the bone behind the ears. This is where two very important neck muscles attach. Between this point and the lower jaw bone, just about below the ear lobe, you can palpate a very sensitive spot. This is the location of the *transverse processes* of the first cervical vertebra, the uppermost joint of the head, our first segment of movement.

4.4 The Ideal Posture of the Upper Body and Head when Riding

Dressage Seat

The upper body of a good rider radiates elegance and calmness. It balances without apparent effort, vertically and horizontally to the horse's back. And no matter what the horse's movements under the rider, the upper body is always part of the movement, as if grown there.

In the riding theory we can find observation criteria for the assessment of the upper body posture. We should be able to draw a perpendicular line through the points of ear, shoulder joint and hip joint. This basically resembles the description of the little tower of the building blocks: pelvis, thorax and head. The tower is most stable when all blocks are arranged exactly on top of each other. When looking closely, we can see that the upper body is never totally still but incorporates itself into the movement of the horse. Another

frequently applied rule says that the hips of horse and rider as well as the shoulders of the two should always be arranged parallel to each other. This can be observed in tight turns or during a significant lateral bend of the horse. It means that the rider should always adjust their upper body to the direction of movement. In the riding theory, this is described as the natural

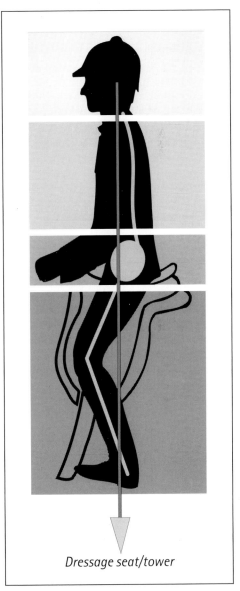

Dressage seat/tower

position of shoulders and hips in a turn.

Forward Seat

In the forward seat the upper body leaves the perpendicular line, and is tilted forward. This tilting happens exclusively in the hip joints. The spine does not alter its position. The individual building blocks of pelvis, thorax and head maintain their position in line with each other. Only when in this position can the complicated interplay of the muscles of the trunk function automatically. Concurrent with the tilt forward, the weight is balanced over thigh and knee. Your own centre of gravity should coincide with the centre of gravity of the horse. How far the upper body is inclined forward, and how much contact the seat has with the saddle, depends on the individual situation and the horse. The forward seat is thus a dynamic and adaptable seat, which can adjust very well and very quickly to the most diverse movements of the horse. Therefore, when developing more speed in the canter, when galloping or jumping, the forward seat is a must for rider and horse.

Forward seat: balance and lever

The forward seat should always have a forward tendency. Getting behind the movement is fatal for the balance of horse and rider.

4.5 Unmounted Exercises: Upper Body and Head

In order to feel the erectness of our own bodies, it would be helpful to sit in front of a mirror, since our own backs are often more alien to us than our little toes, which we can at least see. Thus the mirror is a very helpful control instrument. The main problem when correcting the posture is getting more and more stiff and cramped while consciously trying to adjust it. Incomprehensibly, we start feeling more and more unwell. If you encounter difficulties with one of the following exercises, take a break, move about a little and try again.

The perception of your own body is a further problem when trying to correct the posture. Lie down on your back and try to lie perfectly straight. The longer you think about it the less sure you will probably become as to where the straight centre line is. The feel of body and movement depends also on the duration of a position. This can be compared to the sensation of warmth. Imagine three glasses of water, with hot in one, lukewarm in the second and cold water in the third. When immersing both index fingers simultaneously from the cold and the hot glass into the lukewarm glass, the sensation will be very different. One finger will regard it as relatively cold, the other as relatively warm. The *perception of your own body* is therefore not a measurable fixed quantity but a relative perception. A stimulus, applied to a joint for a long period of time, will initially be distinctly perceived, but then the perception will diminish. For example, after assuming a crooked osition for an extended time, the actual straight position will be perceived as rooked. Lie down on your back and take a alf moon position. When lying straight gain after a few minutes one side of the ody will appear a lot longer.

Vhy this long excursion? Owing to the pinal column, the upper body is a very exible structure: it is very difficult to gain ontrol over it, and it is even less easy to alance it during movement.

Now sit down on your stool and repeat the ocking motion of the pelvis (see chapter bout pelvis). Then, when you watch ourself closely, you will realise that the movement of the pelvis causes movement n the entire upper body, like a chain eaction.

Correct erectness of the upper body does not guarantee correct position of the pelvis. But if your pelvis position is not correct you have no chance of achieving a correct posture; it is the basic building block and must be placed correctly. However, even with the correct pelvis position you can have faults further up in the upper body.

How can we feel if the remaining building blocks are aligned properly above the pelvis? Palpate the lower tip of the sternum with one hand and put the other hand on the top of the pubic bone. Now, when rocking on the lower branches of the pelvis you will feel that the distance between your hands diminishes and increases. When increasing, the thoracic cavity becomes automatically erect. At the same time the abdominal muscles become

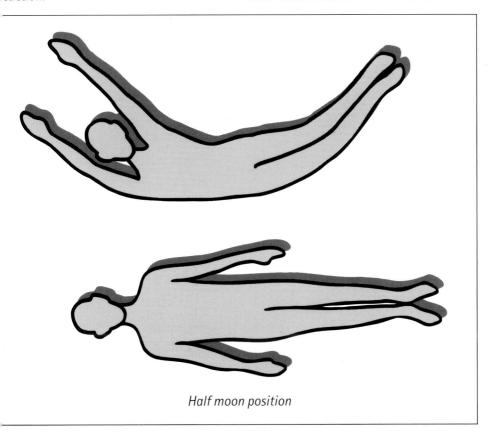

Half moon position

4.

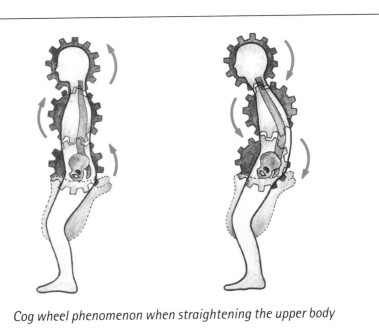

Cog wheel phenomenon when straightening the upper body

longer, another example that the abdominal musculature works toward lengthening, not shortening! But, since the chapter about physiology, you have already eliminated the jack-knife and sit-ups from your exercise programme . . .

When moving the pelvis, the LS makes a flexing and extending movement, which we recognised earlier as the main direction of movement of the LS. The transition to the TS becomes critical since it is better at turning than at flexing and extending. One can frequently observe that a person tips in the LS instead of stretching the TS, and the entire building block thorax is shifted backwards – a frequently occurring incorrect interpretation of erectness. In order to control this, palpate the lower tip of the sternum again, and with the other hand the hollow between the collar bones and the upper end of the sternum. Now execute the same movement with the pelvis once more. You will notice that one hand is pushed forward, then the other. Your thorax is then erect when both hands are perpendicular with each other.

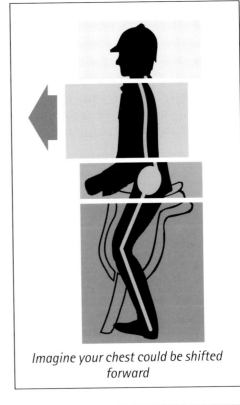

Imagine your chest could be shifted forward

Compare the photos in section 4.6.

A further, but not quite so easy possibility of moving the upper body is a shifting motion. In the process, one building block is shifted to the front or to the side without bringing about any flexing, extending or shifting within the vertebrae.

Put your hands on both ends of the sternum, just like before, and try to shift the thorax to the front, rear or side. Both hands have to remain absolutely perpendicular to each other. Especially important is the shifting to the front. It plays a major part when following the movement of the horse. I recall a remark made by my riding instructor: 'Make your sternum longer, this is actually not possible but ...' and, after the little rider pushed her chest forward 'it is possible!' The image that it is possible to lengthen the sternum like a rubber band is very helpful when

erecting the thorax, without running the danger of tipping in the LS. Another factor for the upper body, which should not be underestimated, is the respiration. The diaphragm has a lot more room when the body is erect and the breaths can flow effortlessly down into the pelvis. I have already emphasised repeatedly how important this is for the interplay of the muscles.

When the posture is erect all building blocks are arranged above each other in a way that makes them stable all by themselves. The muscular support is only minimally necessary. To better understand, put one hand on the back and the other flat on the abdomen.

When leaning forward you can feel how the two long back extenders tighten and how they have to hold the upper body against gravity. When leaning backwards

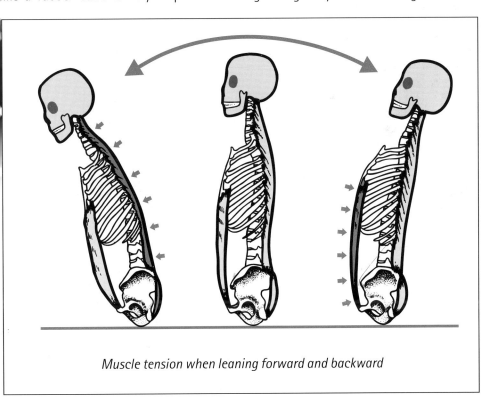

Muscle tension when leaning forward and backward

4.

they relax again, but now the musculature of the abdomen tightens under your hand. The individual middle position of your body would be where the one muscle group is just not yet engaged, while the other is just no longer required. Thus, the upper body is put into a very unstable balance situation. Some time earlier I explained that an unstable balance can produce quick and sensitive movements.

The head has a very important function in this connection. As a rule, it represents a relatively heavy weight (depending on contents) which can upset the balance quite noticeably. Sit erectly, palpate your back musculature and just let your head drop forward. At once you can feel an increase of muscle tension in the back. Your muscular balance is thereby considerably disturbed! When you shift the upper body to the rear, with the head still down, it takes a lot longer for the

abdominal muscles to kick in automatically. The consequence for riding is that a rider who looks down does not possess a sensitively reacting muscular balance in the upper body, and thus gets behind the movement quickly. The head must be carried and balanced freely. In the photos you can study the fatal consequences when the head is held tightly or pushed forward.

The balancing of the upper body above the horse is one of the crucial key points for good riding. The upper body is a system in itself, which is balanced so carefully above the pelvis that it appears to be held perfectly still.

However, balance is not learned by keeping still but by moving. For example, when surfing, the beginners are first taught to capsize the board. The intention is that the pupil kneels on the board and rocks it

Looking down causes the rider to come behind the motion

Forward head position,   *natural position,*   *tucked chin position*

violently. Thus all later necessary balance reactions are taught subconsciously and without fear.

Of course, the rider is not supposed to get his horse to rock, but the fine, small upper body movements are developed through the more exaggerated ones. This makes the connection between the dressage seat and the forward seat clearer. I have frequently observed that the dressage seat of a rider improves considerably after a warm-up phase in the forward seat. A fluid transition from the dressage seat to the forward seat is not as easy as it sounds. It is quite easy to lose balance this way, and the horse will be unbalanced as a result. It is fundamentally important that the upper body is bent forward truly from the hip and that the back does not alter its position; only then can the above mentioned muscle chains of the trunk function automatically.

You can practise this by observing yourself in a mirror from the side. Make sure that you distribute your weight evenly over both feet. When bending forward, the weight on the feet should not change. This is only possible when the seat bones move to the rear. How much you want to flex your knees in the process depends on the length of your legs. A person with a short upper body and long legs will keep the legs

straighter than somebody with a long upper body who will flex the knees more in order to balance a shorter lever. This is quite important regarding the length of the stirrups, but I will get to this later.

It is important to feel to what 'type of bend' you belong. Practise this bending in any possible everyday situation. This is simultaneously a very good training for the back because you bend your back economically and thus save it! You can practise on a bike what this feels like on a horse. Stand up on the pedals and change your upper body position. Then you can feel exactly what happens when you shift your weight increasingly to the front or rear. You can check on yourself in the process and try different positions of the upper body without altering the balance. Every loss of balance triggers a chain of balance reactions which are undesirable for an independent seat and the influence associated with it. During all these small exercises, you will have probably noticed, it is not always so easy to move the upper body into the desired direction. This is partly because you are not accustomed to these movements but also because there exist all these cute little accompanying symptoms such as stiffness, hypermobility, weakness in the posture, crookedness,

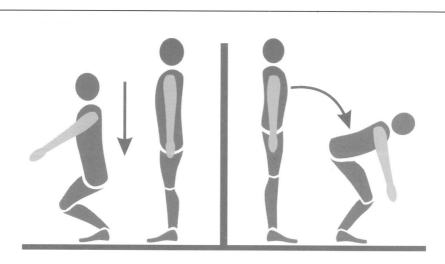

Different ways of bending down

scoliosis (sideways distortion of the spine), muscle tension, shortened muscles . . .

Deficits in the human way of moving are nowadays the order of the day. A good feel for body and movement is not achieved as

a matter of course. Although I try to demonstrate again and again that riding in particular is a sport that can eliminate some of these deficits, some additional gymnastics are usually required. While reading and palpating, you will surely get

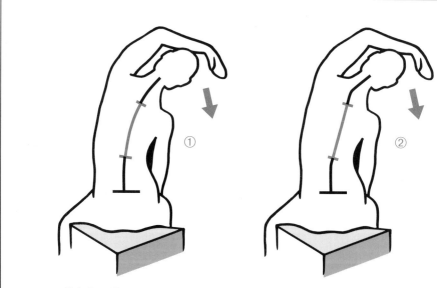

Side bending in smooth arc 1 and with locked thoracic segment 2

to know some of your weak spots. If you feel that you don't get a grip on them, either in your daily activities or in riding, you should consult an expert (Orthopaedic/Physical Therapist).

In the following, I would like to describe a few small exercises which are important for the fine, segmental mobility of the spinal column. In order to improve the mobility of the spine, we should always execute small movements without much effort. When executing extreme extension, the problem spots are simply locked and the movement takes place in the segments located above and below.

The main function of the LS is flexing and extending. You can test and train its mobility with the movement of the pelvis while sitting. To this purpose palpate the spinous processes and feel how the distance between them changes during movement. Or you can get down on all fours and arch and hollow your back.

The TS is the centre of rotation. Thanks to the thorax and the ribs it is a lot more stable and thus allows for the ample mobility of head and pelvis. Flexion and especially extension are therefore more difficult in the TS. In general, we can say that the entire mobility of the TS can be enhanced through an improved ability to turn. When you sit on a chair and, with your arms crossed on your shoulders, turn to the right and to the left, you will quickly find out how easy it is to avoid completing this difficult movement. It is very easy to tilt and shift the upper body. But it is difficult to aim intended movements towards a certain segment of the TS. Therefore the starting position has to be chosen in a way that the body has very little chance of evading the difficulty. In order to improve the erectness of the TS, one should first work on rotation. In nine out of ten cases extension will then be easier to execute.

Sit erect on your stool in front of the mirror. Cross your arms and take a hold of your opposite elbows. Now begin to rock very gently to the right and left. Once you find a good rhythm start lifting the arms slowly until they are about horizontal in front of your shoulders and continue to rock.

The movement of the arms is transferred to

Mobility of the spine on all fours

4.

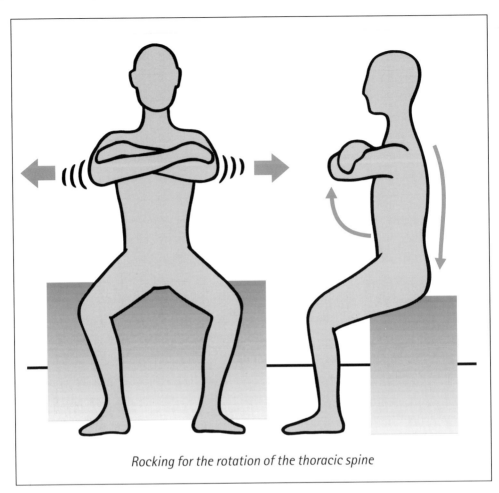

Rocking for the rotation of the thoracic spine

the back. At the beginning the movement produces a subtle rotation located at the upper part of the TS. The higher you lift the arms, the lower this rotational movement slides down the TS. This way you can release one vertebra after the other, and since this soft rocking at the same time loosens tense and cramped muscles it prevents the locking of the problem areas.

In order to improve the extension it is important to put the LS in a flexed position because it is easier to stretch from there, and it is the position one would naturally fall into. Therefore sit on your stool with legs straddled and allow the upper body to

hang forward. Cross your arms behind your neck and start to slowly raise your body, head first. Do you have the feeling that the sternum gets longer and longer and tries to sink lower and lower?

A variation of this exercise would be to put your hands onto a table or a window-sill or to put them against a wall while pushing the stool far enough away that the upper body sinks down until the ears are between the upper arms. Then imagine again that the sternum gets longer and sinks lower.

It is recommended to repeat the rocking motion after such an extension exercise in order to relax the TS and to secure the increase in mobility.

The CS is the most mobile part and I prefer not to give you any specific exercises. One should avoid circular movements since they exert too much pressure onto the sensitive joints, thus causing blockages

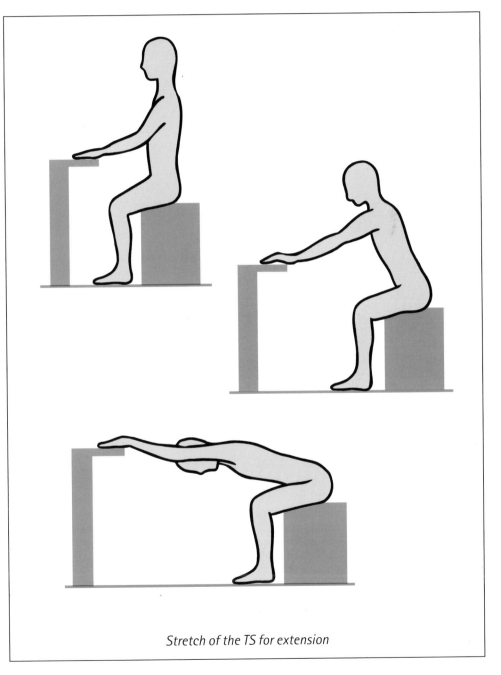

Stretch of the TS for extension

and headaches. If at all, practise the individual directions of the movement 'flexion' until the chin touches the tip of the sternum. The extension should equal approximately the distance between thumb and index finger from the hollow between the collar bones to the chin. The rotation should be about eighty to ninety degrees to each side, and the tilt to the side about forty-five to sixty degrees. The comparison between both sides is more important than extreme mobility. The range of motion should be about the same for both sides.

Once you have your spine and the entire upper body under full control you are allowed to try all of this on top of the horse and during motion. Some things are easier in motion since they are much more natural than all the 'cramped' stretch positions on the stool.

4.6 Balancing the Upper Body with the Movement of the Horse

A stable upper body is the prerequisite for following the horse's movement. Stable does not mean rigid, but rather steady, corresponding to the situation at hand. As explained in section 4.2, the thorax segment represents stability, the head is mobile, and the pelvis is as well and has the task to 'restrain' movements from below and to transfer them in a coordinated way to the spinal column.

When you sit on your horse at the walk try to imagine this stable-mobile feeling. Only when stabilising well in the area of the TS can we let the horse move our pelvis correctly. The thorax should hold the upper body erect in a stable fashion and induce such balance, that the other body segments are enabled to move. Only this way is it possible to swing in the pelvis or

to achieve independent hands.

Imagine again the little tower. Thorax and head are aligned perpendicularly over the balanced pelvis. It is all right to once again palpate the muscles of the back and abdomen. With closed eyes, flex your upper body forward and backward a little, find your own middle position, just like at home on the stool, but now with the movement of the horse. Palpate the upper and lower tip of the sternum and check if these points are vertical to each other and if they remain stable when the horse goes forward. At the walk one can often observe the rocking upper body, with the lower tip of the sternum dropping backward downward. This can never agree with the picture of riding forward! Consciously always try again to lift this lower point, and then try for the tendency to push both

Slouching . . .

arallel to the front. Keep in mind that the iaphragm can not work optimally unless he sternum is in this middle position. Watch other riders and check on yourself, specially during transitions and half halts. Weaknesses of the seat are most obvious t these occasions. Exaggerated reclining r collapsing of the upper body can often e observed.

Once you have built your little upper ody tower, concentrate on the lateral distribution of your weight. Can you feel he basis of your seat, and do you sense ow significant or subtle the movement of he upper body would have to be for hifting the weight?

From the drawing once again observe ow the support area of the body is constructed. The fact that the basis of the eat is triangular does not allow for a true lateral displacement of the weight. On the other hand one can topple over with this 'three-legged stool'. This would be equivalent to a shifting of the weight in three possible directions: to the back, and diagonally forward to the left or right. In the riding theory the latter is often called 'pushing the hip forward downward' or 'increased loading of the inner hip'. For this, also see the chapter about the pelvis. It is important to know and to feel that each lateral shifting of weight is connected with a forward movement. In the process the upper body must be taken as a whole in the direction of the movement. Otherwise you dodge with the spine and your tower collapses. These movements are extremely subtle, otherwise the weight would move to the wrong side, and faults like a collapsed hip

Sternum vertical (natural position), Exaggerated stiff erectness

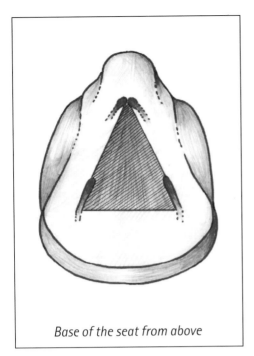

Base of the seat from above

Another exercise, a favourite with children, is the 'hugging'. Bend over forward and put both arms around the horse's neck. The head should lie supply on one side.

With this exercise the whole spine is wonderfully stretched, which most people find very pleasant. In order not to destroy the achieved suppleness and stretch, it is important to take the head up last when returning to the erect posture. First the pelvis should be rolled backward and then one should erect oneself vertebra after vertebra. The hands are allowed to help and push against the horse's neck. This is not an exercise to improve strength, but rather mobility.

Another good exercise is 'patting the horse'. Pat your horse with the right hand

or waist would develop.

Now I would like to show you a few possibilities of how to loosen and stretch your thoracic spine while walking on a long rein. This will help you afterwards to make your upper body erect and to join in the movement of the horse. Earlier I had mentioned that a rotation of the TS from below, just as when walking, facilitates erectness. This means, that while simply riding at the walk, you already receive impulses for an erect posture, since the horse pushes your pelvis from one side to the other, thus rotating the lower part of the TS. Riding at the walk therefore does not only loosen the horse! Close your eyes for a moment and try to feel this rotating movement. To this purpose you can also place a hand on your back and feel the spinous processes with your fingers. Ask yourself then if you really turn equally well to both sides. Often one can discover at this occasion one's better profile and find an explanation for a multitude of seat problems in the upper body balance.

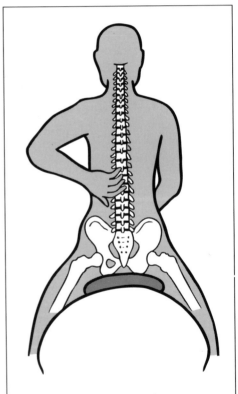

Palpating of the rotational movement at the walk

on the left side of his neck. Make sure that you do not alter your weight above the pelvis. You may lean forward and look at your hand, but the movement should come from the TS, not from the pelvis. Your TS then executes a lateral tilt combined with a bend and rotation to the same side. This three dimensional movement makes use of the entire TS-mobility. Leave your hand at the neck, change the pressure against the neck and, for example at the rising trot, push your hand down a little when sitting down. Compare your right and left side, does this correspond to the previous findings about your upper body?

In order to improve the rotation to one side, put your hand onto the hip bone of the horse. The other hand remains in front of you and the pelvis is supposed to further maintain the balance as the base of the seat and may not follow the rotation. The movement of the horse is cushioned lightly with the arm and you look in the direction of your rear hand. The head should always be allowed to follow the direction of the movement, in this case the rotation, otherwise the danger of blocking individual vertebrae is too great.

At the rising trot one can feel and develop the balance of the upper body. Adjust your stirrups to a medium length for this purpose. Too long a stirrup complicates the balance when leaning forward, too short a stirrup makes the balance more difficult when in the vertical. Fluid transitions between the dressage seat and the forward seat are an important and effective means to improve the fine balance of the dressage seat. The logical connection between all seat forms clearly calls for a versatile basic education. Thus you can improve your upper body balance of the dressage seat by frequently changing into the forward seat. The horse emerges in the process as an excellent teaching master. As soon as you no longer follow the movement or stop

balancing your weight when leaning forward, the balance of the horse becomes affected and he will react accordingly. Therefore, lean your upper body further forward when rising to the trot and take it back again without influencing the gait and suppleness of the horse. Then you can be sure that you were not behind the movement.

Alternating rising and sitting to the trot (also without stirrups!) develops balance and the feel for motion of the upper body.

When riding through turns and at the canter we can feel the lateral displacement of the weight. Feel how each displacement to the side is connected with a tendency to the front, as described above. Now imagine the comparison to walking. When negotiating a turn, stop briefly and check which hip advances and what happens in the opposite shoulder. You will notice that riding puts the same demands on the upper body. The diagonal bracing, the so called *rotation seat*, is therefore not so terribly complicated, but rather a normal way of moving for us, we just have to learn to carry it over to the horse.

A balanced upper body is the basic stability for any influence, any task. A lack of upper body balance can only be compensated through an increase of strength and influence. In the process, joints, especially those of the spinal column, are over stressed, and the horse's balance is frequently disturbed. The harder you work on your upper body balance, the more you know about your problems and strengths, the more effortlessly and beautifully you will ride and your horse will be grateful.

Segmental straightening . . .

Patting – a simple exercise for the rotation of the spine

. . . of the spine

Upper body balance at the rising trot

4.

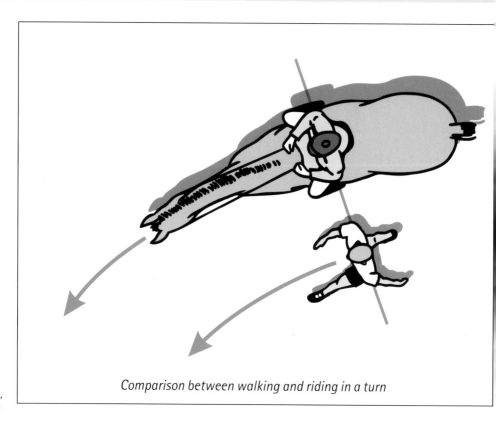

Comparison between walking and riding in a turn

5.

Centre of Independence Shoulder Girdle and Hands

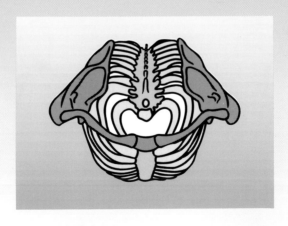

5.

5.1 Anatomy: Bones and Joints, Muscles and Tendons

The *shoulder girdle* consists of the *shoulder joint*, the *shoulder blade* and the *collar bone*. This fine continuous structure is mounted on top of the thoracic cavity, similar to a yoke carried on one's shoulders. As a result, there exists no stable joint connection between the shoulder girdle and the trunk. The collar bone alone possesses a tiny joint with the sternum. This permits the large variety of arm movements. The shoulder girdle can slide on the trunk in all directions.

When you look at the shoulder joint closely, you will realise that the joint socket covers merely a small part of the large ball of the upper arm. This means that the shoulder joint has very little bone guidance – the support of the joint is mainly ensured by muscles. Those joints are in much greater danger of being dislocated than the joints that are, in comparison, tightly secured by bone and ligaments (for example, the hip). When you look at the *elbow joint* further down you can see that the upper arm bone forms a large joint there together with the two bones of the lower arm. This joint is

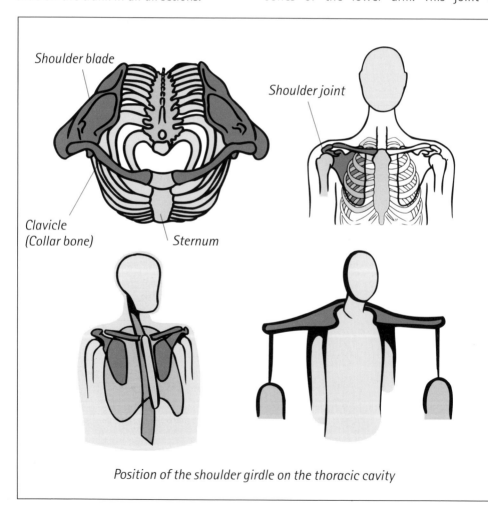

Shoulder blade

Shoulder joint

Clavicle
(Collar bone)

Sternum

Position of the shoulder girdle on the thoracic cavity

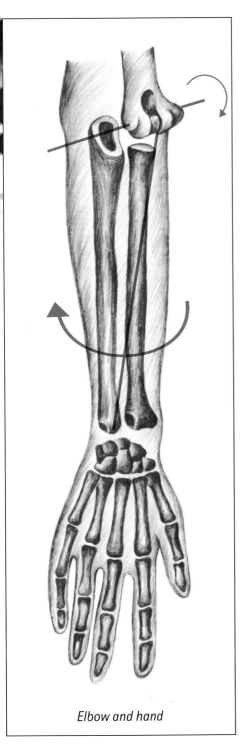

Elbow and hand

capable of flexion and extension and can also perform some kind of rotational movement, the rotation of the lower arm.

The *wrist* has a large number of small bones. These small bones shift among each other during each movement, and it can cause great problems if they catch in any given place. In summary one can say that the shoulder possesses the greatest ability to move in all directions. With the elbow joint one can flex and extend and turn the lower arm to the inside and outside. With the wrist one can mainly flex and extend and move laterally either toward the thumb or the little finger. Due to the multitude of small bones a mixed movement is possible in almost all directions.

I do not want to elaborate on the individual muscles, as they are too complicated.

It is important to know that the shoulder girdle and shoulder joint are mainly secured by muscles.

5.2 Body Proportions and Individual Constitution

Since the shoulder girdle lies like a yoke on top of the thorax, its 'fit' is of critical importance for its mobility. Depending on the length of the collar bones and the shape of the shoulder blade the shoulder girdle can be broad or narrow. With men it is often broader than with women. In order to judge the mobility individually, we should contemplate the width of the thorax as well as the width of the shoulder girdle.

Look around among your acquaintances, and you will certainly see different types of constitution. A narrow shoulder girdle limits the mobility of the entire

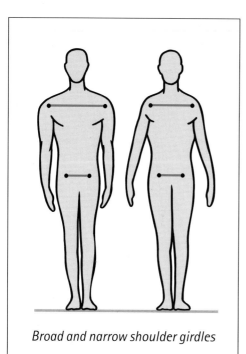

Broad and narrow shoulder girdles

shoulder complex, the arms frequently cannot hang freely and without tension beside the body. Physiotherapists recommend to these individuals that they support the weight of their arms as much as possible, for example, to prop their hands on the hip bones, to put them into trouser pockets or to cross the arms etc. Otherwise the muscles in the back of the head and neck would cramp very quickly. Later I will elaborate the difficulty of carrying one's upper arms supply next to the body when riding if afflicted with this problem. One can also observe big differences regarding the upper arms. The length often varies considerably. Some people can easily reach the iliac crest with their elbows, with others the upper arm ends above the waist at the height of the lower edge of the ribs. This difference in upper arm length becomes relevant for the angulation of the elbow when holding the reins.

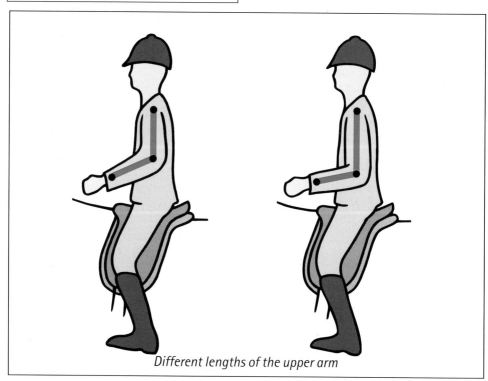

Different lengths of the upper arm

5.3 **Palpating the Most Important Landmarks on the Body**

Now it is your turn again. How well do you know your body at this point?

Before starting to palpate, look at yourself in the mirror:

- What are the contours of your shoulder girdle, is it rather broad or is it narrower than the thorax?
- Are both shoulders at the same height?
- What is the shape of your collar bones?
- How long are your upper arms, how far down do they reach on the sides of your body?

Once you have answered these questions for yourself, trace your fingers along the collar bones, starting at the sternal notch. You can feel that the collar bone has an S-shape and that it ends in a rather broad plate. This is called the *acromion process*. Palpate the outermost edge of the acromion process. There is often a problem corner, when tendons are inflamed or jammed. Proceeding from the acromion process you can palpate the edges of the shoulder blades further back. It is of course harder to palpate oneself in

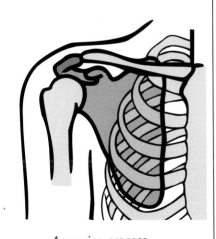

Acromion process

the rear. Either find an assistant to palpate you, or contort yourself to feel the characteristic triangular shape of the shoulder blades.

If you have an assistant available, you can

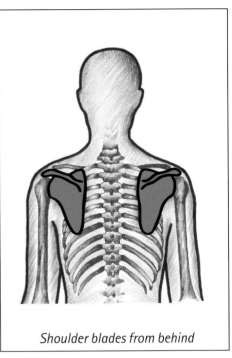

Shoulder blades from behind

compare from behind the distance of the lower tips of the shoulder blades to the spine. Often some asymmetry can be found there – one shoulder is carried farther forward than the other.

At the elbow you can easily palpate the two lateral corners and the tip in between. Between the inner corner and the tip of the elbow you can feel a small groove. It is often very sensitive, an important nerve runs there all the way up to the hand. This is the so-called 'funny bone', you can feel the pain all the way into the small finger when bumping it.

When you palpate the tip of the elbow and then flex and extend the elbow you can feel how this tip disappears during

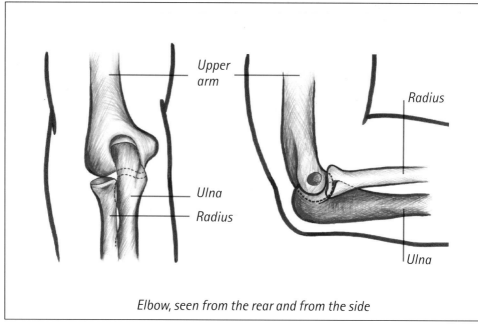

Upper arm

Radius

Ulna
Radius

Ulna

Elbow, seen from the rear and from the side

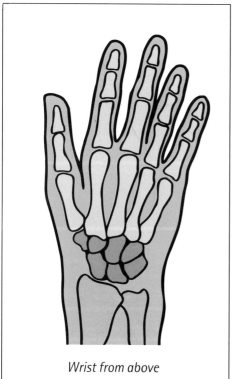

Wrist from above

extension, like clicking into place. The elbow joint is arrested in the extended position and has no more springing ability. You can easily imagine the effect of such an arrested elbow on the mouth of a horse. Independent springing action is no longer possible.

At the wrist you can palpate the lateral bounds very easily as well. Now, palpate about a finger's width further in the direction of the hand. There you can find all the many small bones. Feel those bones from above and below and try to push them up or down, or move your wrist, then you can feel their small movements under your fingers.

The hand is a very sensitive work of nature. How nice it would be if every rider could apply it as such when riding!

5.4 The Ideal Type of Hand Position on the Horse

Dressage Seat

The shoulder girdle should rest on top of the thoracic cavity. Then the upper arms are able to hang freely and supply alongside the upper body. The elbows are slightly angled, the lower arms are carried. The hands are held upright about one hand above the withers, their height depending on the height of the horse's mouth. The line, elbow – hand – horse's mouth, should be perfectly straight when viewed from the side and from above, and, if at all, it may only be broken for a moment either to the outside or upwards.

One should hold the reins with the wrists in a mid position and with closed fingers, without arresting the wrist in the process. The thumb holds the end of the rein down, shaped like a little roof.

Forward Seat

This shoulder-arm position should essentially be maintained in the forward seat. When tilting the upper body forward we have to make sure that the shoulder blades do not slide forward as well, but stay in their place on the trunk. The upper arms may then be taken a little bit further forward, they need not be held close to the upper body any more. But, they should not be spread to the side like 'pot handles' either. The connecting line, elbow – hand – horse's mouth, should remain straight in the forward seat as well. The hands should now be placed at about the middle of the horse's neck and are allowed to contact the neck. The ideal yielding of the hands over a jump should be in the direction of the horse's mouth. However, for a beginner

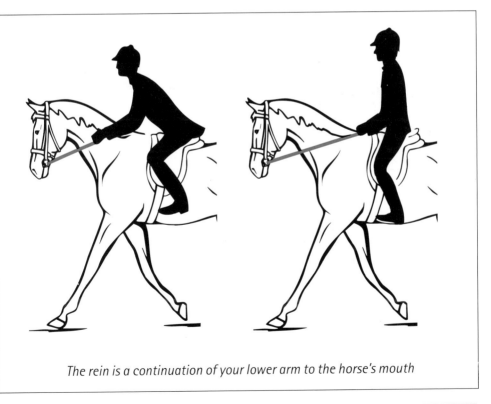

The rein is a continuation of your lower arm to the horse's mouth

Yielding with the hands reins over a jump

Bridging the reins

it is easier at first to hold the hands on top of the neck and slide them forward along the crest when giving the rein.

It is important that the wrists remain relaxed when holding the reins in a mid-joint position alongside the horse's neck. The fingers should be closed around the reins without gripping tensely.

It is very popular to make a bridge with the reins in order to allow the rider a more secure handhold and support.

5.5 Unmounted Exercises: Interplay Trunk – Hands

In the following section I would like to demonstrate how closely the trunk and extremities interact and depend on each other. We should never look at any part of the body by itself, it is important to always

Yielding with the 'bridged reins'

see the entire person, and the individual body segments in their function for the entire organism.

Due to its location on top of the thorax, the shoulder girdle is dependent on the position of the spinal column, especially the TS. You had best sit sideways in front of a mirror, very casually with round pelvis and thorax. The shoulders hang forward, often the head is a little pushed forward as well and the CS quite considerably bent. The correction: 'Take your shoulders back' would have fatal consequences. If you simply take the shoulders back without changing the position of the trunk, you would exert a lot of strength and get all cramped up in the process. You could not endure this position for very long. Therefore, drop the shoulders back down, and start to straighten from the pelvis. Automatically the thorax is lifted upward and forward, and it is like pushing the thorax under the shoulder girdle. Then the building blocks of the upper body are aligned once more and the shoulder girdle can be carried without any muscular effort. In any other position the musculature has to hold the shoulder girdle in place.

It is important to remember that it is not a matter of taking the shoulders back but rather the thorax must be pushed underneath the shoulder girdle, so it can be carried in a relaxed way.

This applies to the dressage seat. In the forward seat the upper body is bent forward and the shoulders would slide forward without muscular support. In the chapter about the upper body I demonstrated how important it is not to change the position of the spine when leaning forward. Here the muscular bracing of the trunk musculature plays a big part. An important muscle group is the *lower fixators of the shoulder blades* which see to it that the shoulder blades maintain their location on the trunk even if the upper body leaves the upright position. If these muscles do not engage or only work insufficiently, the *muscles of the back of*

Sloping shoulders

Straightening in the thoracic spine helps to carry the shoulder girdle freely

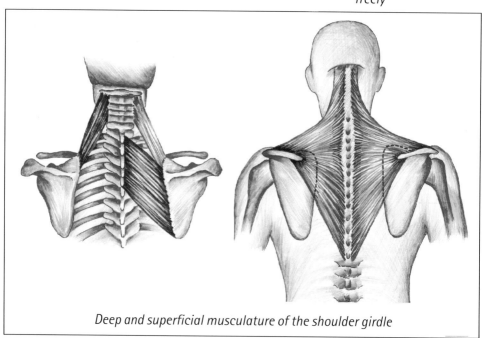

Deep and superficial musculature of the shoulder girdle

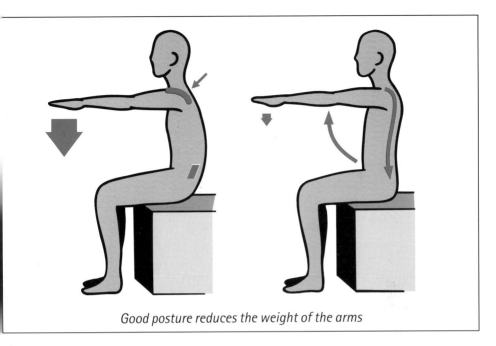

Good posture reduces the weight of the arms

the neck compensate for them, and severe tension in this area is often the result!

If you study the drawing of the deep musculature of the back closely you will recognise that it is feathered like a spruce tree. This very special construction transmits all forces which attack the spine, which is an entire structure of its own, in order not to over-stress a single segment. All theories about helping the back and posture are based on this realisation.

You can feel this very clearly when executing the following exercise: sit down on your stool once more, again casually with a 'crooked' back. Close your eyes and lift both arms to the front, about ninety degrees. Do you feel the weight of your arms? How heavy are they? What part of your body carries them? Where do you feel the most noticeable muscle effort?

Lower the arms again, shake them loose a little, make your upper body from the pelvis up erect and repeat the same exercise, this time with an erect spine. You can clearly feel the difference now, the weight of the arms is now distributed

evenly over the entire back, it appears lighter and no longer attacks one individual segment like a lever.

Now take a look at your shoulder blades, or even better, watch them from behind on your 'assistant'. When lifting the arms, no matter if to the side or to the front, the shoulder blades remain at up to an angle of about ninety degrees. Then they start turning on the trunk forward and upward. They only facilitate large movements. For riding this means that the shoulder blades can remain quietly on the trunk, since the small movements of the shoulder blades required for riding should never exceed an angle of ninety degrees!

With the following exercise you can feel how important the relaxed position of the shoulder girdle is for the entire movement of the arms. Lift your arms, once while your shoulders are pulled up beside your ears and once with them down. Feel the difference in the quality and effort of the movement. Earlier, I mentioned that the

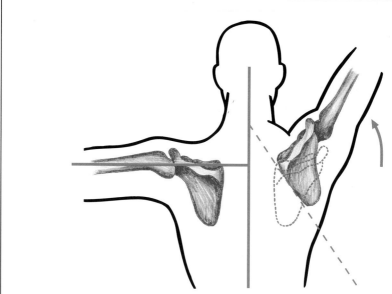

Starting at about ninety degrees the shoulder blade begins to rotate

shoulder joint is guided and secured mostly by muscles. But when all muscles work simultaneously the joint locks, the movement becomes sticky and the joint becomes literally jammed. The acromion process has a very important function here. Look for it one more time in the drawing and palpate it on your own body. If the ball of the upper arm bone is pulled upward while the arm is being lifted, it quickly jams below the acromion process. This can lead to irritation of muscles and tendons, even to inflammation in this area. Calcium deposits are often the consequence and can make most movements of the arms very painful.

The moment you lower your shoulders in the direction of the pelvis, you create an 'air space' below the acromion process, the joint then has more space for all movements. If you are ever told in a riding lesson: 'Shoulders back and down', this means, that you should check the erectness of your upper body, that you should bring your thorax well forward

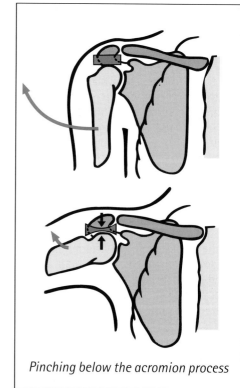

Pinching below the acromion process

under the shoulder girdle and that you should lower your shoulder girdle slightly in the direction of the pelvis.

Why did I describe the function of the shoulder in such detail? Because it is determined here whether the rider's hand can function independently from the horse's movements, or whether the arms have to perform equalising movements for the unbalanced trunk.

In the chapter about physiology I spoke about muscle chains. A muscle never works alone, but always as part of a chain which is supposed to accomplish a certain function. I would like to explore with you two chains that are important for the movement of the arms. Stand up straight and begin to turn your hands to the outside, starting from the thumbs. Keep turning, and you will feel how the following joints become involved in the movement. Elbows and upper arms turn to the outside, the shoulder blades slide backward toward each other, the thoracic cavity becomes erect ... they end in the so-called *stretch pattern*. The opposite happens when you turn the hands, thumbs first, to the inside. Elbows and upper arms turn toward the inside, the shoulders come forward, the spine starts rounding and you end up in the *flexion pattern*; in the extreme you would curl up like a baby. This flexion pattern is a protective reflex one frequently retreats to, for example, when afraid, stressed ...

These muscle chains are very important for riding. When you recall one more time the position of the lower arm and hand, you then recognise it as the beginning of the stretch pattern. The small fingers should be closer to each other than the thumbs, thus the outward rotation is initiated in the body. However, if somebody rides with concealed hands, then the flexion pattern is initiated, and yet one is supposed to erect the trunk.

Two opposing muscle chains run through the body and meet each other in a joint. This is then the critical spot. This joint can no longer cushion a directional movement, the chains break. With the above example we can observe this critical spot mostly in the shoulder or neck area. Thus many tiny, minor details are of great significance for the theory of riding, many small things amount to a lot in the end!

Another small subtlety which has a great impact in the holding of the reins itself. You should take one rein up and try the following right now. If you try to hold the rein firmly with your fist, the wrist immediately becomes very tight, elasticity is then unobtainable. You have to hold the rein between thumb and index finger. Then the fingers can communicate independently with the horse's mouth without having to hold the rein at the same time. The riding theory dictates: 'The thumb lies like a little roof on the rein'.

I know only very few riders who observe this. But try it out. Close your hand to form a fist and press the thumb down flatly. Move the wrist now in various directions and feel how tight it is. Now change the position of the thumb, squeeze down with the same pressure, but this time only with the very tip of the thumb – you will feel that you can move your wrist much more freely. When the thumb is flat one muscle tightens the entire wrist. A small cause with far reaching consequences!

In the chapter about the upper body I demonstrated some exercises for the improvement of the mobility of the spinal column. They are basically the prerequisite for good mobility of the shoulders and arms. Any developing movement is first initiated by the trunk, then the extremities follow. However, there are a few very beneficial stretching exercises just for the shoulder girdle. Our civilised ailment, which is poor posture, especially when sitting, often causes the shoulder girdle to slide forward. This means, in the long run, severe tension in the area of the back of

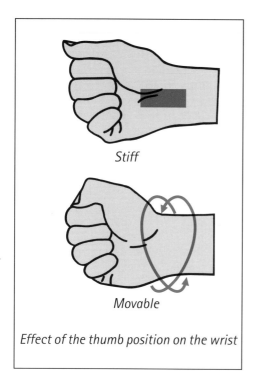

Stiff

Movable

Effect of the thumb position on the wrist

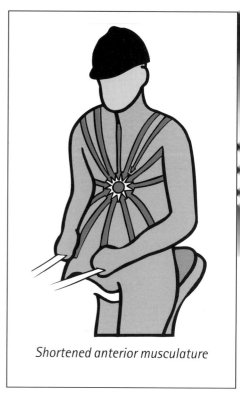

Shortened anterior musculature

the neck, since the shoulder girdle is suspended there on the muscles of the neck instead of resting on the thorax. As a result, the muscles in the front shorten since they are never stretched sufficiently.

You can practise the following exercises very well at a door frame or a wall. It is more important to incorporate them into your day than to do a firmly planned evening exercise programme.

Stand with your side to a wall, and lay the hand closest to the wall behind your body and against it. Your shoulder must touch the wall. Now try to turn the trunk away from the wall, you will then be able to feel the stretch at the shoulders. In order to address all muscle parts the arm should be stretched in different positions. You can execute this exercise by reaching as far down, and working your way as far up, as possible. It is important that the trunk remains close to the wall. Maintain this stretched position for a few breaths and try consciously to direct the breathing

into the stretched area. This aids the muscles to relax and stretch. In order to improve the outward rotation of the shoulders, stand again with your side to a wall, flex the elbow beside the body at a right angle and press with the lower arm (not with the hand) against the wall. Then turn the trunk away from the wall again. The lower arm must not lose contact with the wall. Careful – no cheating by pressing the fingers against the wall while the wrist has lost contact.

Another good exercise for in-between times is to simply hook both thumbs behind the back and to move them backwards away from the trunk. While doing this it is important to keep the thorax erect and not to escape into a bent position.

Finally I would like to show you an exercise to stretch the connective tissue of

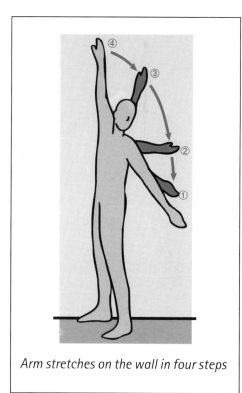

Arm stretches on the wall in four steps

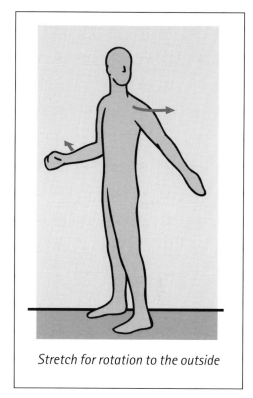

Stretch for rotation to the outside

the collar bone and the neck. As long as things are tight there it is not possible to make the upper body erect in a relaxed way.

Put your hand with the edge of the index finger against the opposite collar bone. The other hand can be laid upon it for assistance. Now slide your hands downward from the collar bone by taking the skin with you and let them lie there while exerting a moderate pressure. Now, move your head diagonally to the back and you can feel the tension in the tissue. The direction in which you want to move your head depends on your individual feel of the stretch. It is only important that you do not start circling the head. First stretch in one direction, return the head to normal and then try a slightly different direction. Breathing can strengthen and improve the stretch of this exercise as well!

A free and independent shoulder girdle

is also of considerable importance for every day well-being. Isn't a person who is feeling well also a better rider?

5.6 The Independent Hands of the Rider

When judging a rider, a very important factor is whether or not they have good hands. Pretty much the worst reproach for a rider is that of hard hands. On the other hand, one is being taught that the rein aids are actually the least important aids and that they may only be applied together with the weight- and leg aids. Why then are soft hands so important for riding?

First one can easily say that the horse's mouth is held sacred by a good rider and that a horse, whose mouth was ruined at some point, will never again approach the

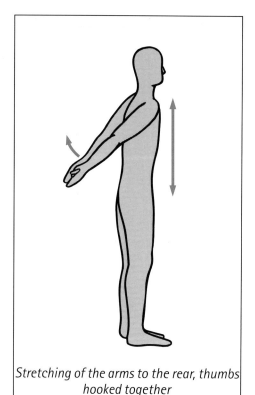

Stretching of the arms to the rear, thumbs hooked together

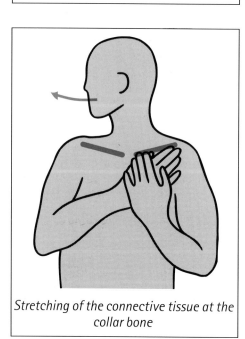

Stretching of the connective tissue at the collar bone

bit unbiasedly and confidently.

Secondly, we can recognise a good rider by their independent hands. As soon as the upper body loses its balance in any way the extremities try to compensate, and the arms very quickly try to help with balancing. Thus, one can infer that a rider with independent hands has a balanced seat. The soft and constant connection between the horse's mouth and the rider's hands is called contact, with the horse establishing this contact by stretching to the bit. This means that the hands of the rider have to adjust to the horse's mouth and may not be put into a certain place without any relation to it. When good hands are very quiet and act very subtly it is the result of the even contact and the fact that the rider has become a part of the horse's movement. But these hands are no more immobile than the rider's seat! Each correction of a riding instructor: 'Hold your hands quiet' is thus a paradox, and mostly results in the opposite.

The popular seat exercises where the rider is asked to hold the hands without reins as still as possible above the withers are therefore totally useless. Even when the rider is experienced their knees would slide up easily and the hands learn not to feel any contact to the front.

In the following I would like to point out some learning steps and possibilities for how to scrutinise the independence of the hands, which are valid not only for beginners. The advanced rider especially sometimes needs a little help in keeping a cool head as well as quiet hands when facing a difficult situation.

A small strap at the pommel of the saddle has proved very helpful. However, the small rings that attach the strap to the saddle are not sturdy enough if holding on in a critical situation, and we can find ourselves none too gently on the ground, strap in hand. Thus, when using a certain saddle regularly for seat exercises it is recommended that a saddler fortify these rings.

I would like to do away firmly with the prejudice that somebody who holds on to the saddle learns to hold on to the reins. Above all, pulling oneself into the saddle is not supposed to aid an independent hand but it is an aid for the stability of the upper body. And I don't think that I have to elaborate any further on the fact that a stable and balanced upper body is the prerequisite for independent hands. It is best to hold this little strap with a hand on either side and then to turn the hands outward as if to try stretching the strap.

Do you still remember the muscle chains mentioned before and the continuous movements? With this small bracing of the hand you have initiated the stretch pattern in your body. As a result, the elbows come

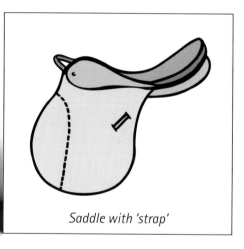

Saddle with 'strap'

with the help of the strap when I ride a difficult horse; as soon as I am sitting deeper I can avoid using a lot of strength and action with the reins.

When pulling yourself into the saddle

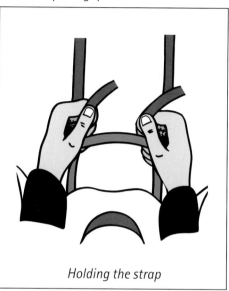

Holding the strap

you have to make sure to hold the strap evenly with both hands. One hand should not pull while the other one is pushing, and the strap should not be loose one moment, tight the next. Here, one can practise the feel for an even pressure of the hands. How firmly the rider has to pull on the strap depends on the stability of his/her upper body. The skilled rider may be able to hold it lightly without any pressure. When a rider is capable of this one can ask him to put tension onto the strap forward and upward. This is not an easy movement. The arms are moved forward while the trunk may not alter its position. Riders often fall forward when taking the hands forward, thus losing their position.

close to the upper body, the upper arms are slightly turned to the outside, the shoulder blades slide backward and the thorax is lifted. When you pull upward on the strap a little, the upper body should not lean backward, but you should feel how the pressure of your seat basis increases. Then, you can achieve a consistent loading of the pelvis with the help of the strap, and this is the most important part of your body which adjusts to the movement of the horse. Even today I save/stabilise my seat

Go ahead and try all those things yourself. It does not always have to be seat exercises on the lunge, even when riding it cannot hurt to concentrate totally on your hands for a few times around the arena. Simply hold the strap together with the reins, either with the small finger alone or with the whole hand. The ordinary pommel strap is often too short. If necessary, you may have to procure a longer one. Then try it not only in the basic gaits but also during transitions like to the trot, to the canter, or back down to a lower gait . . . For example, it is not easy to tighten the strap forward upward while picking up the canter. Many riders tend to pull a little on the inside rein when cantering on, which has nothing to do with the preparatory half-halt. In the process, the inner rein restricts the inner front leg of the horse, and the first canter stride cannot come through freely. Here the strap can be of great help, because the rider can instantly feel himself when his hand is working backwards.

Also when rising to the trot we can check ourselves with the help of the strap. If we succeed in maintaining a constant tension on the strap, the movement of rising is in balance and in harmony with the horse's movement. Another good possibility when rising to the trot is to pat the horse on the neck in the rhythm of the horse's movement. Pat the horse on the opposite side of the neck every time when

sitting down. And when changing hands you should not lose the rhythm either. You can refine this exercise by simply laying the hand on the horse's neck, and instead of patting just slide it a little downward when sitting down. You can also put one hand in the back on the cantle without changing the position of trunk and legs while rising to the trot. Exercises like these help to develop independent arm- and hand movements, and you can apply them then consciously and specifically.

When your trunk is stable, your hands independent, we can start to influence the horse. Fortunately, things are not quite so systematic when riding, otherwise some riders would never be allowed to hold the reins in their hands. For the following exercise you need a bridle, at least a snaffle bit with reins attached, and a partner willing to play the game *mimicking the horse's mouth* with you. Your partner puts their fingers under the bit so they simulate the jaw bone of the horse. Now, you may take up the reins and establish a soft but constant contact.

The width of the reins is quite important. They should be wide enough that they can be comfortably placed on the base section of the ring finger. Thereby you have to consider that the finger joint is closer to the hand than the lines of the skin outline. You can easily palpate the joint yourself by flexing and stretching the finger. Too wide a rein pinches on the fingers, and too narrow a rein can be difficult and strenuous to hold; one should consider this, especially when there is a tendency to tenosynovitis in the lower arm.

Back to the game of mimicking the horse's mouth. Take up the reins and establish a contact. Your partner will undoubtedly tell you that an even pressure on the bit is more pleasant than an on-and-off contact. And this soft basic tension is necessary so that the horse is able to perceive even the

Developing independent hands

smallest change on the bit. When riding, of course, it should not be you who pulls the reins into this basic tension, but rather the horse should be looking for this connection, he should stretch to the bit and step into it, just as outlined by the riding theory.

Once you have established a connection, and the contact to the 'horse's mouth' of your partner feels right, then just imagine that, instead of the rein, in one hand you hold a sponge which you would like to squeeze out. You will then clearly realise how much influence you can achieve with this small movement. The bit is being moved about two centimetres!

With this game you can illustrate to yourself the various subtle nuances when taking up on the rein. It can reach from a soft squeezing of the sponge all the way to turning the wrist inward. When turning the hand inward one must make sure to turn it a little upward as well, in the direction of the opposite shoulder, and that the elbow remains close to the body, otherwise the increased pressure on the rein is lost and the aid does not arrive at the horse's mouth. I avoided the term *half-halt* on purpose because a half-halt always comprises the interplay of all aids, and it

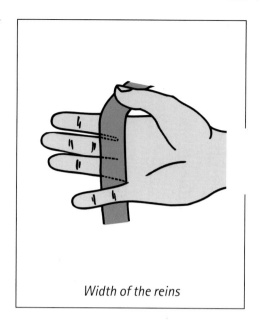

Width of the reins

cannot be practised off the horse.

When playing this mouth game you can clearly feel that the right and left rein are connected with each other. You basically ride with *one* rein which is pulled through the horse's mouth like a sling and connects your hands with each other. As soon as you turn in one hand you can feel the altered pressure in the other hand as well. This should be the same when riding! Ask your

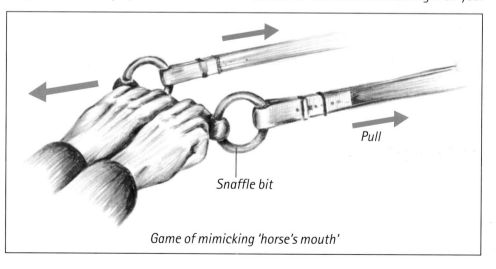

Pull

Snaffle bit

Game of mimicking 'horse's mouth'

Correct position of the whip

Locked wrist with wrong position of the whip

partner if they notice a difference when you take with the outside rein or give with the inside rein! It is amazing how little we think about this. When riding, imagine as well that it is only *one* rein, and you hold both ends in your hands. Then it will be a lot easier in turns, when positioning and bending the horse. Also when riding, as in life, the right hand has to know and respectively feel what the left hand is doing.

You can continue this game with further technical refinements. Exercises like shortening the rein, reins in one hand, changing the whip . . . are examples, and the 'horse's mouth' should not be affected if at all possible.

I would like to say a few words about holding the whip. Of course, the whip hinders the hand, since it is much more difficult to keep the hand upright. The whip should be applied directly behind the

lower leg of the rider in order to support it. Generally the whip has no business at the flank or the croup of the horse. For this reason it should be rested on the thigh. The habit of carrying the whip horizontally is very widespread, but is a very awkward solution since the wrist is bent downward and locked as a result. A springing action is made impossible. However, when holding the whip almost vertically we can turn the wrist around the whip and the springing action remains intact. The whip should always protrude a bit above the hand; it is thus better balanced in the hand and can be swung from the wrist without any effort. The thumb should be positioned around the whip and rest on the rein in the same roof-like fashion. In order not to have to exert any effort when holding the whip, I fastened a rubber stopper on the handle; thus the whip rests on the top of my hand.

Correct hand from the front

One hand across the crest of the neck

And now get on your horse, ride it forward to the bit and push it forward with this one rein as if the reins were poles. Whether you imagine poles or a forward springing rubber band in the process makes no difference, what is important is the feeling of consistently riding forward!

Correct hand from the side

Covered hand

Hand pressed down

Hand too high and stiff

Open fingers

*Uneven length of reins –
hands at different height*

6.

Centre of Balance and Suppleness The Legs

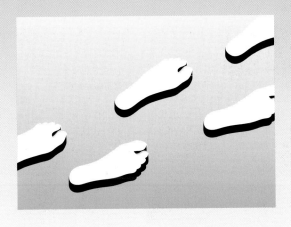

6.

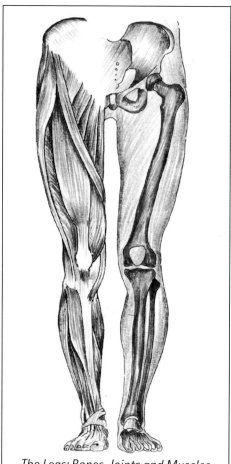

The Legs: Bones, Joints and Muscles

socket. When straddling with the leg, the ball is turned to its full extent below the roof of the socket. This is a position which is especially important for children with hip dysplasia (the socket is not sufficiently developed and the joint is not stressed centrally but rather laterally).

In addition, a firm ligament surrounds the entire joint, it is the strongest ligament of the human body. In comparison with the shoulder, the construction of the hip joint

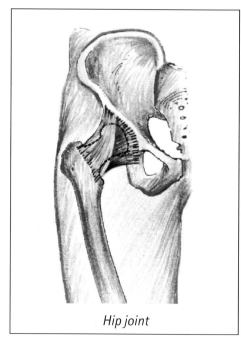

Hip joint

Primarily, the legs facilitate locomotion. This is why the leg joints have a wide range of mobility, thus allowing them to cover a lot of ground. Long muscles, which often extend over several joints, are the movers.

The thigh, shaped especially remarkably, connects with the hip joint at its own characteristic angle. This allows for the tremendous range of movement of the leg. The hip joint is not positioned exactly to the side but rather a little obliquely to the front which is favourable to forward movement. The hip joint is a typical ball joint, the ball is fitted deeply into its

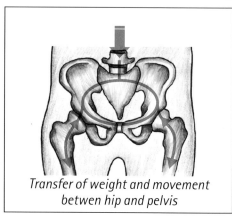

Transfer of weight and movement between hip and pelvis

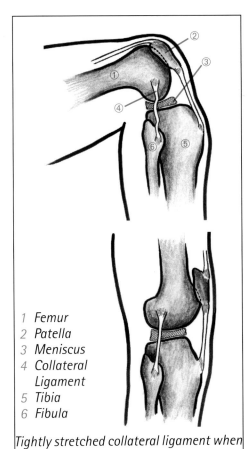

1 Femur
2 Patella
3 Meniscus
4 Collateral
  Ligament
5 Tibia
6 Fibula

Tightly stretched collateral ligament when extending the knee

when extended.

The knee joint consists of the bones of the thigh and the shin. Additional wedge-shaped cartilage discs serve as buffers in the knee joint. Those are the menisci. They help to absorb and evenly distribute pressure in the knee joint, thus saving the joint. The patella is located within a muscle tendon and can slide there. The fibula contacts the tibia laterally. Several muscles attach there, and when tensed, these muscles can be very sensitive to pressure. Further down, tibia and fibula form a fork for the foot. Within this fork the foot can be moved up and down. Since the foot becomes wider to the front the fork becomes tightened when the front of the foot is lifted and relaxed when it is lowered – therefore, when riding, an excessively low heel locks the ankle.

In the lower part of the ankle one can also lift the outer or inner edge of the foot. The tarsal bones are arranged in a similarly complicated way as are the carpal bones. It is interesting that there is another three point support system: heel, small ball and

is a lot more stable. Danger of dislocation is non-existent here. The bone may break, but the joint holds together. The transmission of movement to the pelvic ring takes place in the hip joint. The weight of the upper body is transferred to the legs, and the movement impulses of the legs are transmitted via the pelvis to the spine.

The axis of the thigh is not arranged in a vertical line, but somewhat diagonally toward the knee. This ensures better stability. The main movement of the knee is flexion and extension; in addition it can turn to the outside and inside, but only when in a flexed position since the lateral and crucial ligaments secure the joint

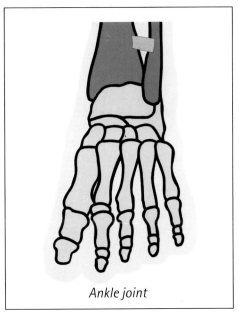

Ankle joint

large ball of the foot.

As you can see in the drawing, the muscles of the legs are arranged in long chains which wrap around joints and bones in a diagonal pattern. Functionally, they can be categorised into groups. For example, the

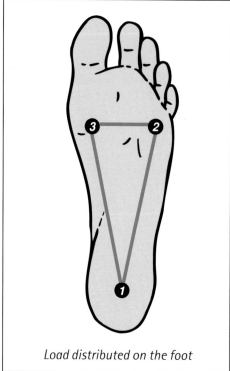

Load distributed on the foot

front musculature of the thigh flexes the hip and at the same time stretches the knee, while the rear muscles stretch the hip and flex the knee. Muscles that extend over several joints are the explanation of why a small movement often triggers a whole chain reaction of consecutive movements. In the following chapters I will discuss the function of the individual muscle chains for riding.

6.2 Body Proportions and Individual Constitution

Leg does not equal leg, and thanks to the mini skirt fashion we can easily observe the multitude of different leg shapes. Long legs, short legs, bow-legs, knock-knees . . . the diversity of variations is quite extensive. Generally, one can say that the upper and lower leg should be about equal in length in order to achieve favourable leverage for the joints.

Another interesting point of observation is the length of the foot. The foot should be exactly as long as the distance from the back of the head to the tip of the nose. Thus the head 'fits' exactly above the feet.

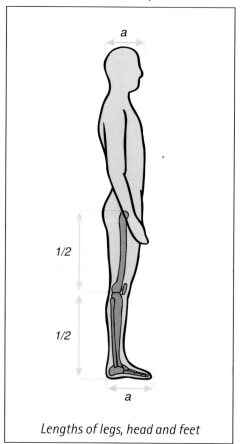

Lengths of legs, head and feet

Only then is the body really in balance. When a person does not carry the head exactly in a straight line above the feet while standing they are not properly balanced. The muscles and joints will have to take care of stability, which in the long run can lead to tension or even deterioration.

The same applies for the dressage seat; a rider is only in good balance when head and feet are correctly arranged.

6.3 Palpating the Important Landmarks on Your Own Body

An important landmark is the lateral hip bone. You felt it already in the chapter about the pelvis. It is located at the height of the hip joint and is therefore of great importance for the observation of movement. This is also where several short hip muscles attach.

The adductors at the inner side of the thigh you already know. Repeat briefly the tightening and relaxing of these muscles in order to familiarise yourself repeatedly with this feeling. Now palpate down to the knee. Feel the outline of the patella and move it in all possible directions while the knee is straight and relaxed. The upward and downward sliding is the most important direction. When extending the knee, the patella slides upward, when flexing the knee, it slides downward. It protects the knee joint. Very tightly-fitting riding breeches can inhibit this sliding mechanism and cause pain in this area, especially when riding for a long time.

Now flex your knee a little and palpate the lower edge of the patella from the side. There you can feel the cleft of the knee joint. With a little practise you can feel the collateral ligaments as well. When you move the knee slightly in the process, you can feel the movement inside the joint. On the outside of the knee, a little further down, you can find the small tip of the fibula. Don't press too hard, it tends to be very sensitive there. As in the elbow, the nerve runs into the lower leg there, and the sinewy ends of the outer leg muscles extend into this area. At the foot you can easily feel the fork of the ankle. You will feel that the inner ankle bone is located a little ahead of the outer one. This explains why the foot, since it moves within this

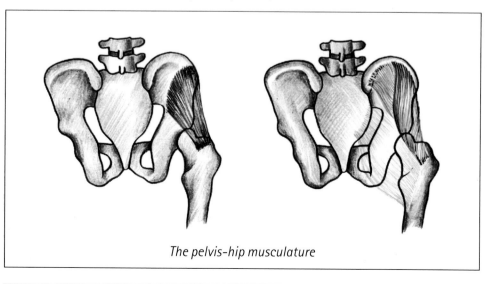

The pelvis-hip musculature

6.

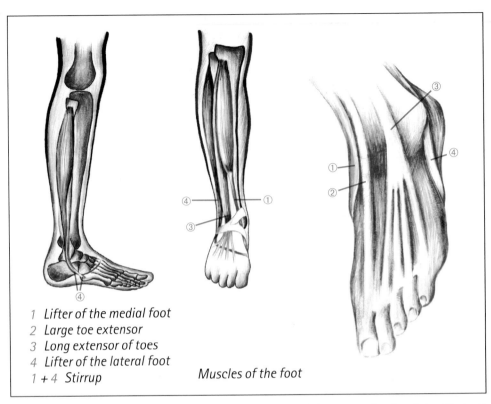

1 Lifter of the medial foot
2 Large toe extensor
3 Long extensor of toes
4 Lifter of the lateral foot
1 + 4 Stirrup   Muscles of the foot

fork, points a little to the outside. How much, depends on the individual position of the joints.

At the foot you can palpate some individual muscles. There are three prominent tendons at the front of the foot. When you pull up the inner edge of the front of your foot, a relatively broad tendon becomes evident there. Relax the foot again and then lift only the large toe: close to the anterior tibialis a thinner tendon becomes evident. Finally lift the toes and the outer edge of the foot, and a third tendon emerges. Another tendon appears laterally below the ankle when you lift the outer edge of the foot. This one is important for riding. It is the counter part of the thick tendon of the anterior tibialis, and in the anatomy these muscles are even called the stirrup since they run below the foot and join together in a sling or, in other words, a stirrup. This outer foot

muscle originates at the tip of the fibula, it is thus the continuation of the outer muscle chain of the thigh.

At the back of the heel you can palpate the Achilles tendon. It constitutes the end of the large calf muscle and its ability to stretch is of great importance for an elastic ankle joint.

Now palpate again the ball of the foot at its widest place. You will notice that the ball of the foot does not point straight to the front, but somewhat obliquely to the outside. The stirrup which lies below the ball of the foot, should be held accordingly.

/pe of Position of the ot when Riding

Forward Seat

The leg should hang down from a relaxed hip joint. At the same time the thigh is taken back and turned slightly inward, as far as the hip will allow without becoming locked. With this motion one achieves the low and flat-lying knee. The knee joint is slightly angled, and the ankle is located in a line below the hip joint. The calf lies flat on the horse's belly, the driving leg on the girth, the supporting leg one hand behind the girth. The stirrup is held just in front of the widest part of the ball of the foot. Then the horse's movement can be cushioned in all joints, which is evident in an elastic heel.

Owing to the shorter stirrup, the hip joints and knee joints are flexed more acutely in the forward seat. The degree of the hip flexion also depends on the degree of the forward inclination of the upper body. Accordingly, the knee is placed further forward on the saddle. The weight of the rider is balanced over the thigh and knee. The lower legs maintain the contact with the horse's body on the girth through the flat-lying calves. The stirrup may be held just a little further back, at the widest part of the ball of the foot, in order to allow the rider more stability. In the forward seat the movement of the horse is absorbed and cushioned in all joints down to and including the heels. Owing to the increased weight-bearing of the legs, this is not as

Correct leg position in dressage and when jumping

easily noticeable as with the dressage seat where legs hang comparatively freely.

6.5 Unmounted Exercises: Interplay Trunk – Legs

In the chapter about the pelvis, we discussed the hip joint and you also located it by palpating. Now I would like to illustrate how much all the small joints and control stations of the body interact.

You learned about the effect of the continuous movements when discussing the arms. On the legs, we find similar muscle chains. With the arms, the outward rotation led to the stretch pattern – with the legs it is exactly the opposite. Turning the legs inward leads to extension, turning the legs outward triggers the flexion pattern. Therefore it is not unexpected that the stretched dressage seat requires a slightly turned-in leg.

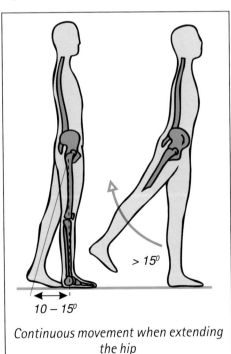

Continuous movement when extending the hip

Now stand with your side to a mirror. Palpate the spinous processes of the LS with one hand and with the other hand the A.S.I.S. of the iliac crest in the front. Now move the leg on this side to the back. After a short distance you will feel that the spinous processes disappear below your fingers and that the A.S.I.S. move forward and downward. First you initiated the extension of the hip and, as sequential movements followed, a tilt of the pelvis to the front and an extension in the LS.

The amount you can extend the hip is quite small. A ten degree extension should be possible without the movement continuing into the LS. It is very important to train the feel for an isolated hip extension. Repeat the movement one more time and watch your leg in the mirror. The lower leg will be about a hand's width behind the other leg. The hip extension is closely related to the supporting leg! If you take back only the lower leg, the rear tendons of the knee would tighten and a relaxed knee joint would thus no longer be possible. Besides you pull the heel up, and the stirrup may be lost . . .

Another important movement in the hip is the rotation to the inside. Stand up straight and palpate the widest point on the side of your pelvis. There you can feel the hip bone. When you turn the leg slightly to the inside now, this point moves to the front, when turning the leg to the outside, it moves backward.

Since the hip joint points a little obliquely to the front, the base of the seat is enlarged when turning the legs inward and diminished when the legs are turned to the outside. You can feel this well while standing. Put both hands underneath your seat bones. Now, you turn the heels toward each other and then the toes. Below your hands you can feel how the seat bones move away from each other while you turn the legs to the inside and come closer

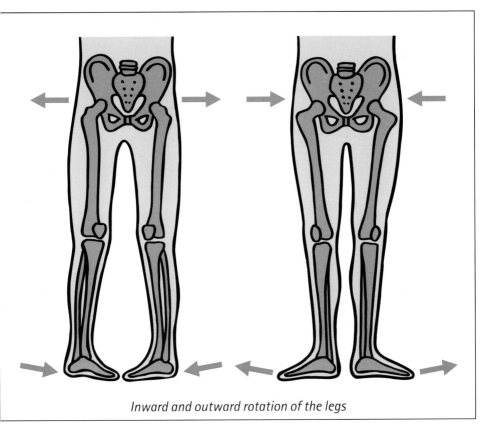

Inward and outward rotation of the legs

together when turning the legs to the outside.

How do we stretch the hip and turn it inward without tightening the large muscle of the buttocks in the process? Stand straight again, distribute your weight evenly over both legs and palpate the A.S.I.S. on both sides. From there you slide your fingers about one inch sideways and downward. Now, try to turn both heels simultaneously to the outside. Below your fingers you will feel a muscle belly pop up. This muscle has a very small belly, and it ends in a sinewy cord which runs along the outside of the thigh across the knee-joint to the tip of of the fibula. With the help of this muscle, you can activate the entire outer muscle chain. Try to feel this muscle again and again, in different positions, when walking, when sitting, when walking up and down stairs and, of course, when riding. This outer muscle chain helps to get the knee closer to the horse, and it also aids in lifting the outer edge of the foot.

Most of the hip muscles extend over the knee joint as well. Therefore, a locked hip joint usually causes a locked knee. The slight flexion of the knee which is required when riding is equivalent to the neutral position, which means a position where the joint capsule is most relaxed and the joint cavity has optimum space, and as a result there is only minimal pressure within the joint. In this position the muscles are in balance, and a springing action of the knee is possible.

Now, sit down on a stool and angle the knee at about ninety degrees. The foot is

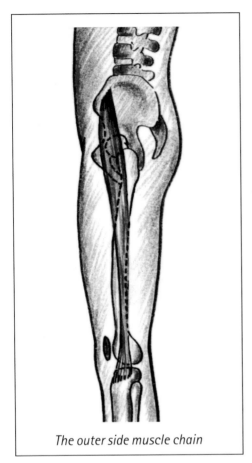

The outer side muscle chain

meniscus.

When riding, mounting is a critical moment. Riders with knee problems often experience pain when mounting, since the knee is extended and rotated from a flexed position. One way to avoid this is to mount facing forward. However, with big horses you would have to stand too far to the rear, and all the horse would have to do is take one step forward ... Therefore, when mounting in the classical way, one should be sure to first push one's weight up with the knee straight before rotating it. Or you can use a mounting block and then the knee is secured.

It is important to remember that an extended position of the knee locks the joint thus immediately affecting neighbouring joints. In the dressage seat, an extremely stretched down leg prohibits suppleness.

When standing evenly on both legs, your knee joints should still have about half an inch of stretch to spare toward the rear. Many people stand with knees overly stretched, hyper-extended toward the rear. Standing this way reduces support by muscles, and relies on the suspension by ligaments. The knee capsule is put under traction, and the joint cannot be nourished properly. In addition, it is harder for the vessels to pump blood back to the heart, a possible cause for varicose veins and swollen ankles when standing for a prolonged time ...

Now, palpate the spinous processes of your LS and hyper-extend your knees several times in a sudden way. You will then feel jerky movements in your LS. When hyper-extending the knee, the thigh is pulled backwards and thus the hip extended. Also the hip flexor is extended in the groin, which counteracts this motion, and since it also attaches at the fourth lumbar vertebra, it pulls this vertebra to

below the knee joint. Now, put both hands sideways into the crevice of the joint, and when you turn the foot to the outside and inside you can feel this movement below your fingers. Stretch the knee and repeat the same movement with the foot. You can no longer feel any movement under your fingers; the rotation takes place in the hip since the ligaments lock the knee when it is extended.

The knee can be rotated when in a flexed position, but not when extended. It can easily lead to injury when trying to stretch and rotate the knee suddenly from a flexed position. It is a typical cause of injury, especially in skiing accidents. The result is ruptured ligaments, tearing of the

he front into a hollow back.

iny impediments, especially posture
habits, can lead to serious back problems
in the lower spine! Therefore, check the
position of your knee joints again and
again in your every day routine, and
whenever you catch yourselves in the
seemingly comfortable hyper-extended
position, change it! Your back will thank
you for it.

Now we will work our way further
down. The foot is a similarly complicated
structure to the hand, and when regarding

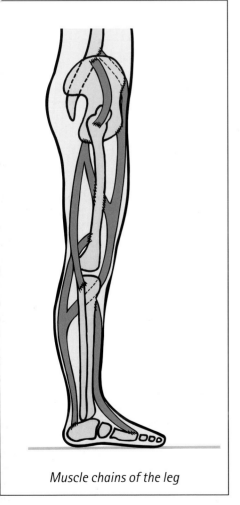

Muscle chains of the leg

the size of the foot, consider that this
small foot bears and balances the entire
weight of the body. We have to
acknowledge that this is a major
accomplishment. Look once more at the
anatomical drawing of the foot. Sit down
on your stool again and take one foot into
your hands. Try to hold the foot as relaxed
as possible and turn it in all possible
directions. The foot is very mobile within
itself, thus enabling it to respond quickly
to even the smallest unevenness of terrain
and shifting of weight. It is best to hold the
foot with one hand while the other one
supports the lower leg.

The ankle joint is supposed to be springy,
while the movement is coming from above,
from the back of the horse. How should
this work?

It is best to stand on the curb of a
pavement or on a stair landing. Bend your
knees a little and bounce your weight into
your heels. This would be the same motion
as required in riding, only in this case, you
are supporting your entire body weight
with the front of your feet.

In order to achieve a truly independent
ankle joint, I recommend the following
exercise: sit on your stool again and hold
one knee with both hands, so that the foot
hangs totally free. Now move the foot in
all possible directions without changing
the position of the lower leg. Frequently a
whole muscle chain reacts: when pulling
the foot upward the knee would like to
extend as well. This is a movement quite
frequently observed when giving the
command: 'Heels down!' Instead it should
mean a slight lifting of the front of the
foot, without changing the position of the
lower leg.

The calf should contact the horse in a flat
way, and again and again we can hear the
statement that the tensing and relaxing of
the calf pushes the horse forward. Is this
really the case? The calf muscle is located

in the back of the lower leg and ties into the Achilles tendon at the heel. On top the calf muscle extends into two large strands over the knee joint.

When this muscle is shortened, it pulls the knee into extension and the heel upward! Is this a contradiction to our riding theory? No, as an attentive reader, you will remember that I already discussed the working of muscles by lengthening them. This is especially the case with the calf. Sit on your stool, hold your knee with one hand and with the other feel the inside of your calf. Now lift the front of the foot, and you can feel how the calf muscle

becomes firmer during this stretch. This downward yielding of the heel is what is meant when asking for a springy ankle joint. As already mentioned earlier, one can practise this nicely on a curb or a stair landing.

However, the leg muscles in particular have the tendency to tighten and shorten – this is mostly due to wrong weight distribution over the feet, hyper-extended knees, and other posture and movement problems. In the following, I would like to demonstrate a few stretching exercises for the most typical muscle chains. Should you encounter extreme difficulties or discover noticeable differences between both sides, it is advisable to consult an expert to search for the cause of this.

For each stretching exercise to be discussed follow these guidelines: assume the stretch position slowly and gently, hold it for several breaths, eventually practise tensing and relaxing while still in the stretch position, and then slowly and softly give it up. Otherwise the muscles will rebound like a rubber band, which can be unpleasant. Bouncing at the end of the movement damages the muscle and leads to renewed shortening!

The gluteus muscles: Lie down on your back and angle one leg with hip and knee at ninety degrees. The other leg should remain stretched on the floor. Now turn the calf toward yourself to the inside, and with both hands pull knee and lower leg in the direction of the opposite shoulder. A slight tugging pain in the buttock area confirms the correctness of the stretch.

The adductors: You are lying on your back again, this time you angle both legs. Now put the soles of your feet together and let the knees drop outward. Depending on the angulation of the legs, different parts of the inner thigh musculature are being

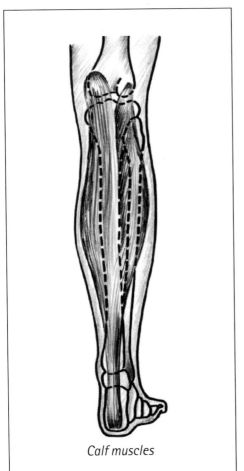

Calf muscles

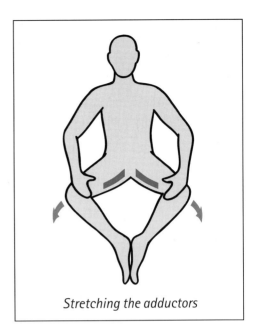

Stretching the adductors

Stretching the gluteus muscles

stretched. The combination of tightening and relaxing the muscles is practised well in this stretch position. Push your LS firmly against the floor and try to gradually lower your knees as much as possible toward the outside. You may also massage the firm muscle cords gently with your hands.

The anterior hip musculature: The most simple stretch is done lying on the back again, one leg is pulled as tightly as possible with the knee toward the abdomen, and the hands fold it there firmly. The pelvis should follow the rotation a little and the LS should be rounded and in contact with the floor. The forefoot of the other leg is pulled upward and the whole leg is being stretched in its entire length, starting from the heel. The exercise is correct when you feel a stretch in the bend of the groin.

Since some of the hip muscles extend over the knee, you can intensify this exercise by flexing the knee of the stretched leg. When lying on your back, as described above, you would then have to lie at the edge of a table or bench so you can let the stretched leg hang down. Otherwise you would have to lie on your side. The upper leg is then maximally flexed, and the lower leg, with the knee flexed, is stretched toward the back.

In order to intensify the stretch, you can loop a towel around your foot and pull on it. It makes little sense to pull the heel toward the buttocks when standing up, since it is too easy to collapse into a

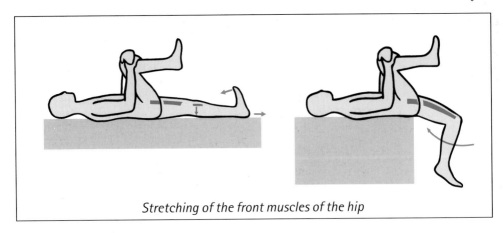

Stretching of the front muscles of the hip

hollow back. For any stretching of the hip, it is important that the other leg be moved in the opposite direction in order to eliminate the continuing movements of pelvis and spine.

The posterior thigh musculature: These muscles tend to be the most contracted ones. Since they are very strong and have a major impact on the position of the pelvis when standing, walking and sitting, the stretching of this musculature is one of the most important. But, do not try to touch the ground with both hands while standing. In this case you stretch the LS, but never fully include the desired musculature. Again, it is important to arrange the legs in opposite starting positions in order to counteract evasive movements. This can be well accomplished when lying on the back. You stretch one leg and keep it firmly on the floor. The other leg you pull with the knee as close as possible toward your abdomen. You can push the foot through a sling, made from a towel, and then try to pull the lower leg slowly over your head, while stretching the knee somewhat. If you straighten the knee at an angle of ninety degrees, you will feel the stretch of the tendons at the back of the knee. It is better to flex the thigh beyond the ninety degrees, then you can feel the stretch deeper in the thigh itself. Muscle tissue is always more elastic than tendon tissue.

The calf musculature: This stretch is important for riding since the yielding of

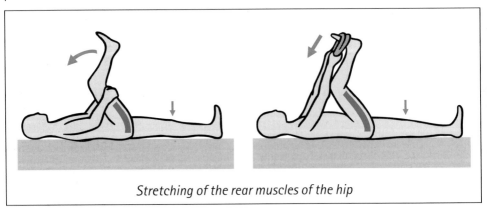

Stretching of the rear muscles of the hip

the calf is instrumental for pushing the horse forward. Stand in front of a wall, with one leg in front of the other in a walking position. Shift your weight onto the forward leg and push your hands against the wall. It is important to observe that the hips remain parallel and that the heel of the rearward leg remains in contact with the floor.

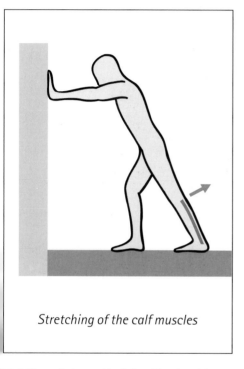

Stretching of the calf muscles

Mobility of the ankle joint: The heel bone has an important function for the mobility of the foot. In order for the heel to be springy, it needs to have some leeway downward. With one hand, grip your lower leg, with the other your heel, and try to move the heel a little downward and to both sides. You will observe that the forefoot is lifted a little when pulling the heel down. This movement happens when riding and is called the 'springy ankle joint'. It is only possible when the foot is relaxed.

6.6 The Position of the Leg While the Horse is Moving

Just as shoulder-girdle and hands must be independent from the seat, a similar independence is asked from the legs as well. The independently hanging leg can be of great help for the balance of the trunk, comparable to the pendulum of a bicyclist on the high-wire.

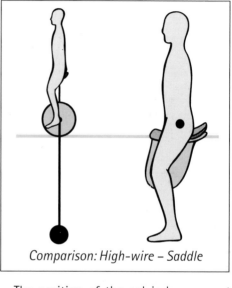

Comparison: High-wire – Saddle

The position of the pelvis has a great influence on the suppleness of the leg. The hip joint is located higher than the seat bones, and it moves inevitably with every movement of the pelvis. The leg was an important aid for finding the neutral position of the pelvis. If the pelvis is tilted too far to the front, one is sitting more on the inside of the thigh musculature. This musculature reflexively tightens when the pelvis is tilting to the rear, thus creating the tendency for the knees to slide up, and the anterior thigh muscle to get tight. Only with the pelvis in the neutral position, can the thigh hang absolutely free. It is an important aspect for good leg aids to develop this feeling and to think about it again and again, especially when moving. On the other hand, the thigh can help

Pulling back of the thigh muscle

stabilise the position of the pelvis; it is thus a stabiliser, while the lower leg is agile and gives the aids.

Get onto your horse and try to create the feel of the hanging leg. At first it will be easier to do this without stirrups. It is not easy to rotate the thigh to the inside and put it flatly against the saddle. It often helps to grip the rear muscle mass with your hand and pull it backwards. Then, the bone comes closer to the saddle, without interfering with the muscles in between. This is an aid which is especially useful for short and round thighs.

Once you feel that your leg is hanging, carefully pick up the stirrup, without losing the feel of the hanging leg. This is not so easy – often the foot becomes a little tense, the lower leg creeps imperceptibly forward, and so the hanging leg is lost. Therefore, it is easier for beginner riders to develop the deep seat without stirrups. Stirrups make it harder to totally relax the legs. But on the other hand, they are of help as well. They carry the forefoot, thus enabling the ankle joint to become springy and allow better contact between the calf and the body of the horse. When you have a good feel for the stirrups, you can check on your own leg position. According to general directions, the ankle joint should be positioned exactly below the hip joint. In order to check on this, one has to look down to the side or have a mirror in the

Lower leg pushed forward

Correct position of the lower leg

Lower leg too far back, stirrup too far in front

'Dancing' stirrup as a self check

afraid of losing the stirrup. As a result they push down onto the stirrup to ensure that it stays put. Such a rider instantly lifts themself out of the deep seat, and the hip joints are locked. An elastic following movement with the seat is no longer possible. It is quite difficult to get along with those stirrups down there. A good exercise is to intentionally lose the stirrups once in a while. Then, when you lift the forefoot, the stirrup often falls back in place all by itself. This playful game helps to overcome the fear of losing the stirrup, and makes clear that the stirrup finds and keeps its place on its own when the leg is in the correct position. The rider does not need to hold it in place. A word of caution: if the stirrup is just long enough to hit the elbow of the horse, it can cause considerable pain to the horse.

It is not so easy to determine the correct length of the stirrups. On my own saddle, my stirrup length differs by six holes, depending on how I intend to ride and with which horse. There are approximate guide lines, but the optimal length we have to find for ourselves. The main criterion for the correct stirrup length is the elasticity of the seat. Too long a stirrup overtaxes the elasticity of the hip, then the rider can no longer cushion the movement there, he becomes stiff. Or, he will try to recapture the stirrup by stretching the foot. In the process, the lower leg slides backward and the rider approaches the fork seat. Too short a stirrup leads to the chair seat, or an increased standing in the stirrups, which in turn tightens the hip through the corresponding muscle chains.

arena. The stirrup is affixed to the saddle so that it hangs on its own, exactly where it should be, which is under the ball of the foot. Now, if you lift your fore part of the foot from the stirrup and it remains exactly in place, then your leg is correct. If the stirrup slides back to the arch, your lower leg was too far in front, and if it slides underneath the large toe, your leg was too far back.

This type of self check is possible at any time during a movement. 'Dancing' with the sole of the foot over the stirrup helps to control the position of the leg and to keep the ankle joint supple. But it is important that you lift only the fore part of the foot, the knee may not be moved upwards under any circumstances. Thus this exercise not only develops the position of the lower leg, but the independence of lower leg and upper leg as well.

Many riders, beginners in particular, are

Experience shows that it is easier for the beginner to ride with somewhat shorter stirrups, since a correctly stretched leg burdens the overall balance too much. Children and beginner riders should frequently ride without stirrups in order to learn the feel for a deep seat. However, care must be taken that they do not clamp their legs tight or pull up their knees. Once

6.

Clamping with knee and lower leg

The careful adjustment of the stirrups is the prerequisite for a supple and elastic seat. At this point I can only advise good care of tack. Since the left stirrup leather becomes longer due to mounting, it is advisable to exchange the leathers regularly, or to mount as often from the right. Try the latter, then you will remember again what it feels like to be a beginner. The absolutely even length of the stirrup leathers is a prerequisite for a symmetrical seat. Frequently riders excuse their asymmetrical seat due to the different length of legs, and reinforce this by adjusting their stirrups unevenly. This would only apply with legs which are at least two centimetres different, and these people generally wear shoes which equalise the difference. Smaller differences are equalised in the pelvis and do not require correction. If you have the feel of sitting continuously to one side, it does not help to change the length of the stirrup on one side. This only creates a false symmetry where the horse is considerably bothered in its balance. You should rather work on your upper body balance. Small rotational restrictions in the spine can lead to evasions through the pelvis.

a person learns to avoid the movement of the horse by standing in the stirrup, they will have great difficulty learning a deep and closed seat. A typical example occurs within a whole nation. In Britain most people have a fantastic forward seat. But in dressage, many riders have problems sitting deep and relaxed.

In dressage, the stirrup should be adjusted so that it finds its own place by the rider merely lifting the front of the foot. This can vary even during one session. I know many riders who adjust the stirrups one or two holes shorter for the warm-up phase, until their own joints get supple, when the hips are better able to stretch; during the course of the hour, it becomes possible to ride with a longer stirrup. Check your own stirrup length, change the length and try to feel the effect on your entire seat. The variation of one hole can sometimes make a world of difference.

One very good way of checking the length of the stirrups is to fold them up toward the saddle flap. The saddle flaps are always cut to the same length. Thus it is easier to compare the length of the stirrups more accurately than when estimating their length by eye from the front. Sources of error, such as a not quite centrally placed saddle, can thus be eliminated. If the left stirrup seems to feel longer after mounting the horse, you should step down firmly on the right one and check the tightness of the girth. Good tack is the tool for good riding. A one-sidedly worn saddle, or a saddle worn at the back usually renders a supple hip impossible.

For trail riding and jumping the stirrups are adjusted shorter to begin with. The

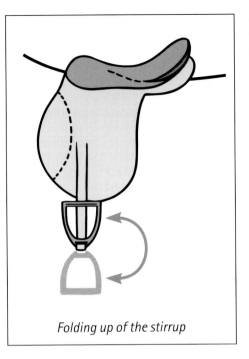

Folding up of the stirrup

anything but easy. On the contrary! It constitutes a differentiated mixture of sitting in the saddle and standing up in the saddle as in the forward seat. Watch a multitude of riders rising to the trot, and pay special attention to their leg positions. With certainty you will see very different pictures. They are all caused by the balance of the rider. As soon as the rider comes just minimally behind the motion of his/her horse, balance compensations take place in the legs, which in turn inhibit a coordinated application of the aids.

For the rising trot, you have to shift your centre of gravity further toward the front since the plumb-line does not run through the ankle joint as in the dressage seat, but rather through the ball of the foot. This can be a tiny, hardly perceptible shifting of weight. With closed eyes, stand evenly on both feet and shift your weight from your heels to the front of your feet. Feel how this is possible with only a very small movement of the body. Precise shifting of weight like this is required for riding.

increased angulation in hip and knee is meant to afford better balance at a higher speed, and to distribute the weight of the rider to the sides of the horse. In the process the centres of gravity of horse and rider come closer together. It is permissible to hold the stirrup a little further back on the foot to guarantee a more secure hold, but the elasticity of the ankle joint needs to be maintained.

I have mentioned, so often, the springy ankle joint, that it surely must be clear to you that this ankle joint is of major importance. It is the last link of a chain, and an ankle joint can only be springy when pelvis and hip and knee joints are supple. In this respect a springy ankle joint is an important observation criterion for the evaluation of the seat. In order to achieve this springy ankle joint, the rider has to allow the movement of the horse to descend down into the leg.

We can feel and learn this very well when rising to the trot. Correct rising trot is

Practise this on the horse also. Stand a little in the stirrups and try to balance. You will notice that this is not so easy, especially during forward movement. You can feel if you are in front or behind the motion of the horse. The knee plays a key role here. You have to manage distributing your weight over your thighs and knees, not just stand in the stirrups. If you merely stand in the stirrups, you have no secure hold. The stirrup is not a firm element, it suspends from the saddle like a pendulum, and therefore does not always remain hanging in the same place. The knee should control the balance in a slightly flexed position. If you straighten the knee you will instantly notice how this disturbs the balance – a frequent mistake when learning how to rise to the trot. The rider thinks about getting up, and the knees are already straight . . .

When rising to the trot, the rising

motion is not measured by the actual height of getting up, but rather by the movement of the hip joints. The upward thrust of the horse's back determines how far the rider rises out of the saddle. When sitting, you may under no circumstances think of sitting down onto a chair – immediately your upper body is too far back, the legs slide forward, balance is lost. A person rising to the trot like this actually works the upper body like a lever against the legs. Not a very pleasant movement, either for the horse or for the rider. Simply let your legs glide lower when sitting down in the saddle. The knee may slide a little downward, but never upward. Then the movement can spring all the way down into the ankle joint. At the beginning, this movement appears so minimal, you might think it impossible to influence the horse this way. And how quickly you acquire a bumping lower leg, far away from the horse's belly when rising, and clamp with a pulled-up knee when sitting. Such a leg may be able to impress the horse, but it possesses absolutely no independence for differentiating the aids.

At the rising trot, the movement flows down into the heel at every other stride of the horse; at the sitting trot this happens at each stride. Trot your horse and pull yourself into the saddle in a way that you load the base of your seat consistently. Then you can concentrate on your legs alone. When you truly let your legs hang you can feel that they become a little longer each time the horse's feet hit the ground. It is important to allow this.

Above, I discussed how the thigh stabilises the seat and that the lower leg is independent and responsible for applying aids. Unfortunately, it is a common mistake, especially of the outside lower leg, to slide forward and thus not be in position for the intended task. I would like to describe a few pictures, in the hope that they will help to keep the lower leg in place: imagine your leg is a bow whose string extends from the hip joint to the ankle joint. A slight tension runs along the front of the thigh and over the knee as the lower leg is taken back a little. Look once more at the drawing of the anatomy – indeed, the thigh muscle extends over the knee. When riding, it needs to become (once more) longer, and not shorter.

Another picture is of a rubber band that extends from your heel to the horse's hind foot on the same side. After all, this is the leg your lower leg should be influencing.

Try both pictures when riding. And always practise them during forward motion, because this is where you need it. The seat is not static!

The position of the lower leg becomes more important during turns and half-halts. Also, at the canter strike off we can often observe the inner leg sliding forward during the landing phase of the stride, thus not being ready to initiate the next canter stride. Pick up the canter and try to feel the contact of your calf against the horse at all times. Imagine the pictures during the landing phase to ensure the correct position of your lower leg. So far, I have endlessly discussed the position of the legs, but never mentioned how to apply the aids. This was intentional, because the horse can pick up his own aids from a correctly positioned leg. When the hind leg swings forward, the ribs on the same side are pushed forward as well, and as a result the horse's body comes closer to the rider's leg . . .

This is of course the ideal situation. We often accomplish this feeling only for brief moments. But it is very important to monitor constantly the strength involved while applying aids. We should strive to reduce it to a minimum. Here, I would like to warn of a too technical application of the leg aids. With every leg aid, the whole seat reacts as well! The driving leg at the girth is in position when you allow the leg to hang as discussed. For the supporting leg, and when retracting it, start at the hip

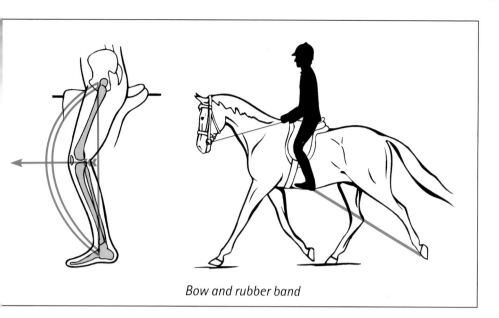

Bow and rubber band

- it is a very small movement, and often riding a turn is in itself sufficient to place the leg there. For example, you are on the right rein and are riding through a corner: in the turn your inner hip is pushed forward by the pelvis – your weight is placed increasingly onto the inner branch of your pubic bone. Automatically, the outside hip is stretched more and the outside leg assumes the supporting position. If you really are in balance and are following the motion, many things happen by themselves. You have to picture this feeling again and again, until these very special moments turn into longer periods and you can finally maintain it for several times around the arena. Here is a tip for harmonising your aids: if, for example, you would like to trot on and the horse does not react to subtle aids, repeat them instantly with a lot more energy. Afterward, immediately repeat the lesson with the more subtle aids. Most horses react more sensitively the second time. A horse can only react with sensitivity if it is concentrating on the task. Riding without applying much strength requires lots of concentration from horse and rider alike. If

you exert a constant pressure with your leg, your horse will get used to it. You will need more and more strength. Compare this with the following picture: put your hand onto your thigh with pressure. To begin, you perceive this pressure a lot more clearly. After some time, you get used to this pressure, and your perception makes room for other things. But if your hand contacts your thigh only very lightly and taps it once in a while, your perception is directed time and again toward your thigh. The short and light pressure is a lot more expressive than a long continuing stimulus which is easy to get used to. It is the same for the horse.

Once your horse has reacted to your trot-on aids, let your legs hang again immediately. The horse will perceive this as reward. It will remember that the pressure onto its side ceases as soon as it reacts to it.

During movement, the legs are supposed to embrace the horse. The breathing leg on the horse's body is mentioned often enough. Basically this is supposed to describe the correct suppleness of the leg. It is always in place in order

Correct position of the lower leg

Lower leg rolled inward

Lower leg turned to the outside

to urge the horse on, if necessary, and to maintain diligence and concentration. It is a treat to ride a horse that is really on the leg and thus initiates its own aids. To make a horse this sensitive is a question of concentration and great patience. Not all that easy, but very worth while!

Supporting leg

Wrong application of the outside, supporting leg

7.

Perfect Body Coordination – Application of the Aids

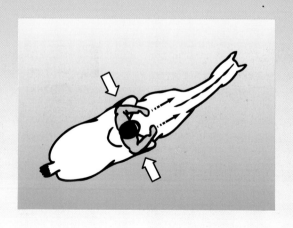

Effect and Influence of the Rider's Weight on the Back of the Horse

The aids are divided into weight-, leg- and rein-aids and they need to be systematically learned by heart. One knows how to use the weight aids by loading one side more or both sides equally, how to aid the horse by taking the weight out of the saddle, one knows about the driving leg, the supporting leg, the forward-sideways driving leg, the giving and taking of the reins, the supporting rein and the sustaining hand. One knows of course, in theory, that all these aids have to be harmonised with each other, and that this intricate interplay of the aids is called the 'feel' of the rider. In this book I would like to dispense with the systematic classification of the aids and rather write about the feel. The intention of this book is to present possibilities and ways in which to learn about feeling.

It's not so easy to learn how to apply aids correctly. To begin with, there is the learning of technical movement, like turning the wrist inward. When to do this, how much of it to do and for how long to sustain it – this feel is a knack and its acquisition is a critical step in a rider's development. The weight aids play a key role in this process. They cannot be dispensed with. You can take the legs off the horse or drop the reins, but not even magic can make the weight disappear which you bring with you into the saddle. You can shift it around, but 150 pounds remain 150 pounds and have to be carried by the horse. At this point, I would like to remind you of the picture of the rucksack. The actual pound for pound weight has less significance for carrying the load than how it is distributed and fastened. Thus a small and fine-boned horse may find a heavy rider more pleasant than a comparatively lighter but unbalanced rider.

The weight is always there, no matter what. Your goal is to balance your weight above the horse in a manner in which you always follow the motion of the horse, and become a part of the horse. If the rider is ahead or behind the motion of the horse, the balance of the horse is severely compromised. The natural rhythm of the horse will be disturbed. Equally bothersome is the lateral shifting of the centre of gravity. The horse has to respond to this new weight situation and does so by stepping laterally below the weight or avoiding the weight by escaping to the opposite side. Looking at it from this perspective, riding is a major balance game. When the rider alters weight even minimally the horse has to react. This subtle shifting of weight is hardly evident from the ground, since the horse reacts with lightning speed to regain a common balance with the rider.

The next time you ride your horse, sit very consciously and try to feel if your weight truly follows the motion of your horse at all times, if you feel constantly in balance. Consider the length of lever that your upper body represents – then you can surely understand the impact your head can have if you incline it a little to the front or to the side.

Fluid Transition and Interplay between Dressage Seat and Forward Seat

As described above, weight and thus balance are of major importance for riding, and for this reason I would like to explore in more detail the balancing of the weight in the various seats. It is in the dressage seat that the most subtle balance reactions take place. The upper body is held seemingly immobile. It is balanced around an imaginary plumb-line. The seat basis of the pelvis serves as support base. A triangular support base is quite stable. The legs, hanging from the hips, act like a pendulum and aid in stabilising the balance.

In the forward seat, the upper body is balanced over the legs. There is a higher basic tension in the upper body because the forward seat, owing to its forward inclination, is more unstable than the dressage seat where all the 'building blocks' are arranged on top of each other. This higher basic tension also allows quicker adjustment and reaction to the motion of the horse. The support base of the forward seat is thigh – knee – stirrup. This support base is broader than in the dressage seat. Looking at it this way, we can compare the forward seat with a straddle-legged stance and the dressage seat with a ballet-like tiptoe stance.

At the first glance, the forward seat appears to be the more stable seat since its support base is broader. But when you look at the weight distribution over the support base, the forward seat resembles the letter 'T'. The upper body is a horizontal lever which needs balancing. The support base is broad from side to side, but narrow from front to rear. The unstable position of the upper body requires a higher basic tension and a quicker reaction response of the muscles, which is especially necessary when riding cross country, over jumps and at high speed.

The dressage seat could be compared to the letter 'I' which is fixed to the wall with a thumb-tack through its middle. The support base is small but triangular, and is located in the middle of the body. A vertical body which is balanced by fixing its middle will, like a pendulum, always return to a vertical balance. As far as this balance situation is concerned, the dressage seat is considerably more stable than the forward seat. Experience supports this when watching a cowboy at the rodeo. The upper body has to stay vertical, only then can he stay on. And I am sure you

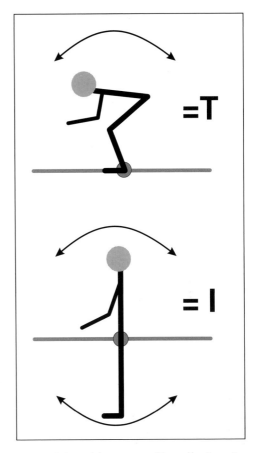

have felt this yourself occasionally: moderate bucking while in forward motion can be compensated for quite easily when standing in the stirrups. But once a horse starts to buck in earnest, you are well advised to sit up straight and to pull yourself deep into the saddle. Otherwise you lose balance and off you go.

In conclusion we can say that the dressage seat has a narrow, triangular and higher placed support base where the legs act as a pendulum. The equilibrium is quite stable, the basic tension of the musculature lower. In the forward seat, the support base is broader but lower, the seat more unstable, with a higher basic tension and reaction response required from the musculature. This is why the forward seat is quite strenuous and needs careful and progressive training.

The transition from one seat to the other is a highly complex movement and balance exercise: to change from a tall and narrow to a broad and low support base, and to constantly adjust the basic tension of the musculature to the situation without getting tense. This task is especially suited to training your own body awareness. Having to adjust again and again to a new situation helps to train your own subconsciously-occurring balance reactions and balance reflexes. The more a rider practises this, the easier they will find their balance on top of the moving horse.

7.3 The Rising Trot – A Difficult Balancing Act

The rising trot is a mixture of loading and unloading of the horse's back. The rider continuously changes support base. After all you have read so far, you will understand what an exacting movement this requires. In connection with the springy ankle joint, I've talked to some degree about the technique of the rising trot. It is important to know and to feel that the rising trot doesn't merely consist of rising and sitting down. The support base changes continuously from narrow to broad, from high to low, from stable to unstable . . .

In the rising trot, many basis seat and balance problems can be diagnosed. The upper body should remain as quiet as possible during the rising trot. Leaning forward while rising and leaning back when sitting down is a very common mistake and unbalances horse and rider alike. One simply is not quick enough to follow the horse's motion in the process. This can also be compared to the upper body balance when sitting down and getting up from a low chair. If you want to get up from a low chair with the upper body upright, the weight of your body is behind your feet; you can only accomplish this by using your arms and a good amount of momentum. It is quite similar when sitting down. When the weight is too far back, you can no longer balance the last few inches and you plop down into the chair. Only if the upper body is tilted forward to a degree where the weight is evenly balanced above the feet can we sit down and get up in a controlled way. A person who is able to check this motion at any given moment without losing equilibrium is correctly balanced. Stopping and maintaining this segment of a movement is another way of examining balance.

At the rising trot, the plumb-line does not run through the ankle joint but through the ball of the foot. This corresponds to distributing the weight over the front of the feet when standing. How far the upper body needs to be inclined forward or how vertical it may remain, varies. On a horse in good self carriage with a more collected gait it will be easier to maintain a nearly vertical upper body in contrast to a young horse that is ridden long and low. Of course, the rider shouldn't be too far forward which would bring the horse onto his forehand.

Our own body proportions play quite an important role at the rising trot. Think of the different 'types of bending over' which I discussed in the chapter about the upper body. Someone with long legs and a short trunk is more likely to lean forward when bending over while a person with a long trunk will remain more upright. At the rising trot, the length of the thigh is of special importance. A long thigh requires more forward inclination than a relatively short thigh.

Only when successful in balancing the trunk above the changing and moving support base can the hands maintain an

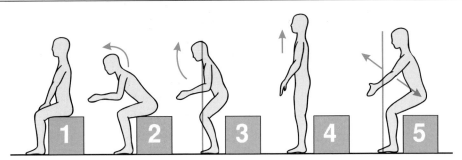

1–4 Getting up in good balance – feet remain in line with the centre of gravity
5 The centre of gravity remains behind the feet

even contact with the horse's mouth, independent from the motion of rising up and sitting down. Observe different riders during the rising trot. The habit of raising the hands when rising, and lowering the hands when sitting down is quite prevalent. You can practise this again nicely with your little strap at the pommel of the saddle. During each phase of the rising trot you should be able to maintain an even and light contact in any desired direction (preferably forward and upward); never should the tension of the strap change or even go slack.

The legs should neither clamp nor stick out during the rising trot. The habit of standing in the stirrups, as well as the attempt to rise exaggeratedly with the help of too tightly gripping knees prevents the fine

Correct rising trot in good alignment

*Unbalanced rising ahead of the motion –
clamping with knee and lower leg*

Overly straight and exaggerated rise

*'Pushing the pelvis through the arms' –
locked hips*

Rising with an unflexed knee

Rising behind the motion

Sitting down behind the motion

balancing above the moving support base. You may have difficulty imagining that the support base slides lower while you are rising up, and that when sitting down the legs become longer and the seat deeper, but the support base is coming up a little. However, once you understand and feel it on the horse, it will appear very logical to you.

7.4 The Rider as Initiator of the Horse's Movement

In order to get the horse to move, the rider has to follow the motion of the horse. To create a picture-perfect model on top of the horse at a standstill is useless for riding. First of all the rider has to learn to become part of the motion which they intend to initiate momentarily. I would like to explain this through the example of asking the horse for canter.

A beginner who does not know what the canter feels like will hardly be able to apply the correct aids for the canter strike off. The more often a rider canters a horse, the more their body learns to adjust to the changing motion, until they are finally able to influence it voluntarily. When I make a student on the lunge canter on from the trot for the twentieth time, the horse usually knows after the third time that it is supposed to canter on as soon as it perceives any change from his rider. Often the students complain that the horse canters on before the aids were applied. In reality the horse was just quicker and more perceptive, reacting to the smallest change as an aid for the canter while the rider was still sorting our their legs . . . This is a good opportunity to teach the rider about varying dosages of the aids. If the horse concentrates and understands the demand, the most subtle aids are sufficient to achieve the desired result. On the other

hand, if the horse had just been going around the ring for half an hour at a lazy jog trot, possibly with an unbalanced rider on top, then it would take a much greater effort to ask the horse to canter.

Back to the example of the countless trot-canter transitions. At first the rider will certainly be behind the motion of the horse, then they will learn to react more quickly until they are able to follow the motion of the horse and to feel when and how the horse's back changes during the transition. Their weight will always be balanced vertically to the horse. Eventually, the rider develops subtle and harmonious aids for the canter strike off. If the rider was confronted continuously with an unfavourable situation for the canter strike off, they could learn only much cruder aids. In the above strike-off scenario the horse is initially quicker during the transition, then the rider follows the changed motion. At step two they remain a part of the motion, and at step three the rider initiates the movement while the horse follows. Horses who take their cues from the seat this way are a pleasure to ride. Basically, it is merely concentration on a mutual balance. I had an unforgettable experience when a very sensitive and nervous horse that I rode constantly resisted going into the canter. The instructor told me that I must under no circumstances close my legs and hold back on the reins, I should merely sit quietly to the trot until the horse took its cues from my seat. It was the only possibility of making this horse listen to and accept the aids.

Children have it a lot easier than adults. They possess very high dexterity and coordination. Instinctively they follow the motion. This is one explanation why so many 'lazy mules' go contentedly forward when ridden by a child. Their balance is not compromised by exaggeratedly applied aids.

It is much harder for an adult to adjust to a moving support base. Just stand on a skate board or put on a pair of roller skates, and you will understand what I am talking about. Children develop their sense of balance all day long. They play, jump, roll, slide ... they seek the challenge, the insecure, in order to understand what they are capable of doing. The adult on the other hand only moves on known territory. Sitting, standing, lying, walking ... the sense of balance is not challenged much this way. But do not worry, it exists and it can be reactivated, just as the child is never totally lost in an adult.

7.5 The Secure Seat

A deep and secure seat is the prerequisite for effective influence. Now what exactly is a *secure seat*? Certainly it has nothing to do with closing the legs tightly around the horse. I know a young woman who was born with only very short leg stumps, but she rides incredibly well with a very secure seat. A rider with a secure seat has eliminated any space between themselves and the horse. They follow the motion in a very balanced and supple way. The entire body is a part of the horse's movements. No outside leg leaves the belly of the horse in a turn, the trunk never attempts to avoid the motion of the horse, the seat is 'glued' to the saddle at any phase of a movement. At no time does the rider open up a loophole, the horse cannot escape, there is no open back door through which the horse can evade the aids.

The more balanced the seat of the rider, the less strength is necessary for maintaining a secure seat. The necessary basic tension of the body is adequate for the required movement, higher at the collected trot than at the walk. Every difficulty balancing the body can only be compensated for by a major expenditure of energy and strength.

Every moment of the horse's movement requires a secure seat. It can clearly be observed and examined during the transition from one gait to another, for example, when trotting on from the seat alone or from a secure forward seat before taking a jump. Even in the forward seat it is very important to have a secure seat. It is more difficult because the balance is more unstable in the forward seat. At the rising trot, it is very difficult to maintain the secure seat unconditionally. Frequently, a rider just closes and opens the seat, and the horse can evade the aids beautifully. The ability to change the load and the support base so that the basic tension is continuously maintained and the rider remains in uninterrupted balance with the horse, is quite an art. Only very few, good riders really master the rising trot to perfection.

7.6 The Secret of 'Bracing the Back'

With all the anatomy mentioned so far, perhaps you have missed the discussion of the 'back muscle' you need for bracing the back, and you may ask yourself why I waited so long to elaborate on this important subject. Now, this back muscle does not exist. The term *'bracing the back'* comprises a matter of such complexity that all the former explanations were necessary to help you understand my view. Look again at the anatomy diagram of the pelvis and repeat for yourself the motion of rolling the pelvis forward and backward. In the process, the seat bones remain in place, and the iliac crest moves to the front and the back. When you stand with slightly flexed knees you can keep the iliac crest still and swing with the seat bones forward and backward. And you can also hold the hips still and move the pelvis around the hips forward and backward. In the process, the iliac crest moves forward and the seat bones backward or vice versa. Now I would like to illustrate that the same movement can look different, depending around which axis the rotation takes place, where something is stable and where there is a mobile region.

Which of the three pelvic movements is important for the bracing of the back?

If we want to push the horse forward by bracing the back, the first version is totally obsolete. Here the weight shifts to the rear (and you want to ride forward!) and the seat bones remain in place. By moving the iliac crest to the rear the LS is being rounded, the fifth lumbar vertebra becomes locked and often the chest sinks down. This means that the motion of the horse cannot be properly absorbed and the upper body is not capable of maintaining a basic tension, never mind increasing it. Unfortunately many riders believe that they can brace the back in this way. In the process they start slouching, and the horse probably receives a bump in the back and loses his rear balance!

With the second version – the iliac crest remains still and the seat bones swing forward – the horse is pushed decidely forward. However, the pelvis lever is very long and requires a lot of strength. Besides, in this position, the fifth lumbar vertebra is pulled again into its locked end position, which influences all movement possibilities of the spine and the trunk.

The third possibility seems the most optimal, where the axis of rotation runs through the hip joints. It makes sense that this movement requires the least effort since we have an upper and lower lever arm. The seat bones push to the front, the movement in the LS is less severe thus enabling the fifth lumbar vertebra to just remain functional. Stand with your side to a mirror and try all three possibilities in order to develop your feel for the different pelvic movements. Feel free to use your hands to stabilise your iliac crest, your hips etc. The upper body should remain as stable as possible. With what do you move now? What muscles are required to work? Basically, it is an interplay of two muscle groups, the abdominal muscles and the lower back muscles.

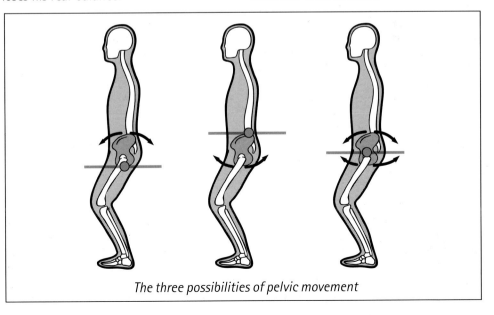

The three possibilities of pelvic movement

The abdominal muscles try to pull up the front of the iliac crest while the back muscles stretch and allow lengthening. You probably recall that lengthening a muscle is the more difficult and strenuous job: an explanation why many riders perspire in the lower back after riding. But this effort alone is not all it takes to brace the back.

With the movement mentioned above, you would sort of slide to the front with the seat bones. But since your seat is 'glued' to the saddle, the forward pressure of the seat bones is transmitted through the saddle onto the horse. By keeping the seat bones firmly on the saddle, there is a danger in executing the first version of pelvic movement, using the seat bones as the stable element and the iliac crest as the mobile part. In order to not evade with the mobile iliac crest to the rear, a stable counter support in the trunk is necessary. Remember, in the chapter about the upper body, I divided the trunk into functional segments where the pelvis was potentially mobile and the thoracic cavity stable. The chest has to create a stable counter support toward the front. This is possible by increasingly erecting the TS, by pushing the sternum forward. For this to happen, the rider has to activate the deep muscles of the shoulder blades and the back (shortening) and the upper abdominal muscles (lengthening).

When, in order to brace the back, you start the movement at the hip joints and stabilise the pelvis upward with help of the thoracic cavity and downward through the seat bones/saddle, the actual movement is very small. Rather, the basic tension of the trunk intensifies, and the increased tension is converted into pressure/energy of the seat toward the front. When movement is visible while bracing the back, the basic tension is diminished and no forward push is created which could be transferred onto the horse. Bracing the back is thus a

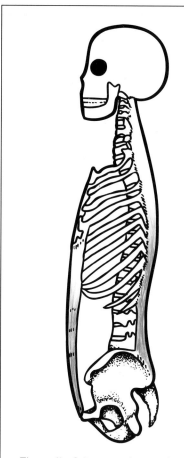

The pull of the muscles on the trunk

question of dexterity and compaction of the seat while in motion, and its effectiveness is independent of the height and weight of the rider.

You can practise this on a stool. Your feet are firmly on the floor and you try the movement of the pelvis, with the upper body not allowing it. In the process, you feel the increase of pressure onto your seat bones toward the front, you could now cause the stool to topple forward. At the same time the feet on the floor offer counter support. When riding, this counter support is provided by the thighs as stabilisers, the lower legs must remain independent.

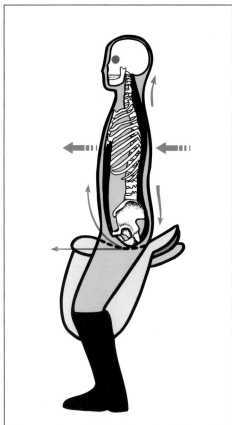

The muscles and their imagined direction of movement when bracing the back

happens automatically, the muscle groups are tuned again to the spinal cord, one can barely influence them voluntarily. You increase your basic tension when you lie down, get up or walk, run, without thinking about that or how you are increasing it. You only know that you would like to get up or run off. These automatisms should be transferred to your riding. Often comparative pictures are helpful. For example, trotting on = walking-running, cantering on = running-skipping, full-halt = stopping from running . . .

I can clearly remember a very talented student who kept plaguing me with questions: 'How do I do this, what does it feel like?' All my descriptions were insufficient. Finally, I escaped into the excuse that this cannot be described, and that some day he would feel it. To him this was not a satisfactory answer, but my firm and confident attitude saved me for a while from further unwelcome questions. Then we had a session on the lunge on a very well schooled and sensitive horse. I let him pick up the trot and canter on his own, ride the transitions without me interfering, I just held the end of the lunge without really lungeing the horse. I asked him to ride transitions from the walk into the trot and canter and back to the walk. The condition was, he had to do it with the seat alone, and without me being able to see any movement from the ground. Soon he succeeded very well, and as he dismounted contentedly, I dared to question how he did it and what it felt like. To my satisfaction I didn't receive a conclusive answer – he said you just feel it. This is the big dilemma with this book. Some feelings you can only feel and are not possible to describe.

The horse is very sensitive toward the basic tension of the rider. Just as he clearly feels when a rider tenses and is afraid, he can clearly recognise a competent rider by their seat. The horse feels the basic tension of the rider and reacts to it. For example, when trotting on, the rider increases their basic tension of the musculature and the horse obeys and trots on. Assuming there is concentration during work between horse and rider and a sensitive application of the aids, one can expect the horse to follow the basic tension of the rider into the requested direction: forward, sideways and backward.

This increase of the basic tension

7.

Driving and Restraining Aids

In theory, riding and especially the sensitive application of the aids always appears logical and simple.

By now, you are equipped with sufficient foreknowledge of the seat so I will try to describe the sensitive application of the aids connected with it. It sounds almost too logical to first perfect the seat before tackling the essential matter, the application of the aids. A student, and even every more advanced rider, is often confronted with a situation where to give aids to the horse is urgently necessary, even if the seat is not 100 percent. Seat and aids always belong together, the more confirmed the seat, the more sensitive the aids can become. The seat itself is a very important aid. The rider always develops both at the same time – seat and influence.

At the beginning of this chapter I mentioned why I consider the application of the aids as a complex situation which challenges the entire rider, and why I do not divide it into the three building blocks weight, leg- and rein aids. I would rather classify them according to their function as driving, collecting and containing aids.

The horse should be contained by the aids of the rider. The British have a nice expression for a horse cantering on the aids: 'between leg and hands'.

Imagine a rubber band or a string you would like to make vibrate. It has to be fixed at both ends, otherwise no vibration is possible. The back of the horse is such a rubber band, and if it is supposed to really swing, both ends need to be fixed. One end is the hind leg that is leaving the ground, the other end the mouth. Not without reason does the riding theory demand that the horse step into the rein. The horse steps up to the bit from behind, and there it rebounds back from the bit, to be better able to develop carrying power. Basically,

this is the function of the driving and restraining aids.

The horse is closed in between the driving and restraining aids. What the rider pushes from behind is caught and measured out in the front. A constant interplay between pushing and restraining aids develops. This interplay of the aids is necessary for each level of training and for each phase of riding. It is just as valid for a young or green horse as for a fully schooled one, and just as important for the suppling as the collecting work. The correction of a spoiled horse has to start exactly at this point. The horse must be secured again between the aids of the rider and through it obedience and acceptance of the aids can be improved.

Work on Suppleness

Allowing the horse to gradually and completely take the reins out of the rider's hands is part of the suppling work and also serves as proof of suppleness. In the process, the horse should stretch forward and downward into the hand. The contact on the reins is maintained, which means, the 'rubber band' remains in tension and the horse's back is able to swing. To ride a horse correctly forward and downward is one of the most difficult things to accomplish in riding. A renowned trainer once said to me that a rider who really understands how to ride the horse forward and downward is just as able to ride two-tempi changes (i.e. flying changes at every second stride). That such a comparison is truly appropriate remains to be seen, but in any case, it points out how challenging this work on suppleness is, both for the horse and the rider.

While being ridden forward and downward, the horse should push off energetically with both hind legs. The back is increasingly arched, and the neck is stretched from the withers forward and downward. This means that the tension of the 'rubber band' increases, in other words, it stretches. At the same time the muscles of the neck and back have to work into becoming longer. (Compare to the muscle work of the rider which I described in the chapter about physiology.) It is of especially high training value to work a muscle into becoming longer! In the theory of sport training, it is said that a muscle can achieve full performance only if it is warmed up and stretched properly. Putting the horse between the driving and restraining aids is here of utmost importance. Without the 'rubber band', a meaningful stretch of the muscle chain from the hind legs all the way to the poll cannot be accomplished. A horse trotting on a loose rein around the ring has no connection with the front. It may warm up to some degree, but its back will not be able to swing.

How far down should a rider stretch the horse's head and neck? There are a few guidelines in the riding theory such as putting the mouth at the height of the point of shoulder . . .

Basically it depends on the situation and the level of training. There are many different ways to design a good programme for the warm-up of the horse. It should always be adjusted individually to the horse, the rider and the current level of training of the horse. I cannot and do not want to give you a generally valid recipe. Instead I will give you suggestions on how to feel yourself deeper into your horse and to find your own suppling programme. And depending on daily circumstances, these need to remain variable. Some horses will relax better on the lunge, others at the rising trot, while some respond better to the canter instead of the trot, some you can supple through half-halts, change of pace and gait, others need work on curved lines, some require a forward canter around a galloping track, some like work over cavalletti, gymnastic jumping or even loose jumping . . . One could add to this list without difficulty. With all these possible variations, it is important to observe that the basic requirements remain the same – stepping to

Riding the horse long and low

Horse on a loose rein

the bit from behind and inter-playing the driving and restraining aids, all of which enable the swinging of the horse's back.

Collecting

Especially for the collecting work, the 'rubber band' is of great importance. During collection, the pushing power of the hindquarters is increasingly transformed into carrying power, as the horse steps further underneath its centre of gravity with increasingly lowered haunches. Due to this increased lowering of the haunches, the forehand becomes lighter and its movement more free. Neck and poll are carried forward/upward and, as a result, the mouth of the horse is approximately at the height of his hip joint. When comparing this to riding the horse forward and downward, the same criteria can be observed. When riding the horse long and low, the back came up, the bow from hindquarters to mouth was put in tension, the entire muscle chain was stretched. There is no difference when collecting the horse, except that the stretch is now directed upward instead of forward. This elevation against gravity, without getting tight in the process, requires a great deal of basic tension (and requires the horse to be closed in between the driving and restraining aids). The 'rubber band' may never lose its arching oscillations. Especially during collection, the oscillations become rather pronounced, and the horse's back moves increasingly up and down as the horse's steps and strides become loftier and more cadenced. This of course requires that the horse is well contained in between pushing and restraining aids, because this relatively high basic tension which is necessary for collection can only be obtained this way, without at the same time losing suppleness and harmony. Often, we can see a backward tendency of the horse's neck and poll during this elevation: these horses evade the stretching and thus sacrifice suppleness. In each phase of riding, and especially during collection, the forward tendency must be evident! This is true also

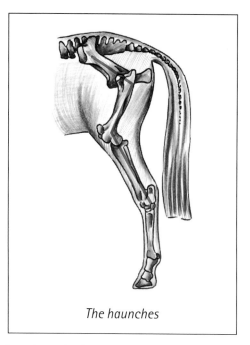

The haunches

decreasing the speed, only for short intervals. Lengthening the strides is a logical counter balance and must be part of the collecting work. If self-carriage and suppleness of the horse are in danger of deteriorating, we should then ride the horse intermittently forward and downward again until it lets go and steps forward into the bit. The interchange of collecting exercises and short intervals of suppling work prevents horses and riders 'becoming tight'. Honest collection needs to be carefully developed.

The rider needs to 'collect' their seat as well. As discussed earlier, the horse can feel the basic tension of the rider and react to it. To collect oneself during riding without clenching is difficult and quite strenuous. Ideally, a rider does not show this effort. Lazy horses, however, seduce the rider into becoming unstable and leaning the upper body backwards behind the vertical, and overly eager horses do not allow the rider to push the horse in the first place, thus inducing them to pull back with the hands. If the seat loses its balance in the process, effectiveness and influence are lost.

for the rein back which is one of the collecting exercises. It tests the obedience and responsiveness and helps the horse to shift his weight to a greater degree onto his haunches.

Another important factor for collecting the horse is that the rider does not restrain the horse merely with the reins but also with the seat. When the naturally elevated horse carries his mouth at about the height of his hip joints, his position provides a very favourable connection between hind legs and mouth.

Whether collection has been truly created by riding the horse with a forward tendency toward the bit can best be proven in lengthenings and extensions. If collection has been correct, the horse can seemingly increase the length of the strides without effort. Prolonged collecting work is very strenuous for the horse. In order to avoid the horse becoming tense and tight, we should ask for collecting work, which is synonymous with

The development of increased basic tension, one's own collection, should be built up slowly. It is understood that a beginner is not able to ride collecting exercises, because they cannot help the horse from the basic seat to develop the necessary basic tension/collection. Therefore it is pointless to ask collection from rider or horse if the muscular prerequisites of either are still in need of development.

An old riding rule says that horse and rider are only ready to work on a curb bit when they are able to execute a correct First Level Test with reins in one hand. At first glance, this sounds a little like military chicanery but, regarded more closely, it contains a whole lot of wisdom. Only when

The dream of collection quite often ends in 'pulling the horse together'

a rider is able with their seat to contain the horse in between their driving and restraining aids in a way that one hand is sufficient to handle both reins, is their basic seat confirmed sufficiently, and are their hands independent and subtle enough to be trusted with a double bridle.

Half-Halts

Half-halts are used for continuous refining and fine tuning of the interplay of the driving and restraining aids.

The most subtle form of a half-halt takes place within a gait. The horse, stepping into the bit from behind, rebounds from the bit, and the series of reactions returns to the back and stimulates the hind leg to step further under the body and to take up more weight. This is the actual sustaining rein aid that the horse retrieves on its own. A rider who has had this fine feel for even just a few moments knows what riding means.

Besides furthering attention and maintaining and improving the gaits, half-halts are also responsible for changing the speed and the transitions between the gaits. I would like to elaborate on the transitions from trot to canter and from walk to trot.

When changing between trot and canter, one mainly trains the horse's suppleness and dexterity. It should happen with good impulsion, and at the same time change from a two beat gait to a three beat gait and a change in the foot-falls

Influence: seemingly effortless

The attempt to engage the hindquarters . . .

. . . ends in a backward movement of horse and rider

The attempt to elevate the horse with the hand . . .

. . . ends on the forehand

without losing the impulsion. This can only happen in harmony when the horse is contained by the rider's aids and the rider's seat is in balance. Horses often avoid the required stretch of the musculature (which I described with the catchword 'rubber band') by raising the poll when cantering on and by lifting the croup during the downward transition, falling onto the forehand, slowing almost to a walk (loss of impulsion!), running off . . . It then takes competent riding through the seat to put the horse calmly back onto the aids so that the transitions can take place once more with good impulsion and suppleness. This exercise is also very useful for testing the rideability of a horse. Basically it serves to supple the horse and to improve dexterity

and flexibility of horse and rider.

The rider learns in the process to change from a parallel loading of their seat base to a diagonal loading and vice versa. A tendency to be in front of the motion or behind it is clearly recognisable in the transition. How many riders get up just a little when cantering on, or fall backward in the downward transition . . . It is a very difficult task to always take one's own centre of gravity into the forward tendency and to remain oneself above the centre of gravity of the horse. Many riders find it helpful to concentrate totally on their seat bones during the downward transition, in other words, at the end of a canter stride to sink deep into the horse, and then load both seat bones evenly and just sit at the

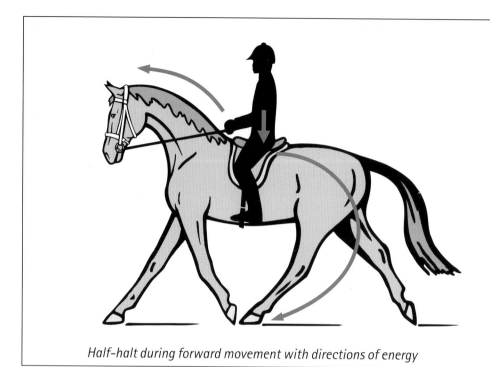

Half-halt during forward movement with directions of energy

trot. It is amazing how little rein influence it takes to slow a horse or ride a transition when trying to use the seat only.

The transition from trot to walk and back to the trot is basically similar to the trot/canter transitions. The main difference is changing from a gait with natural spring and moments of suspension to a gait without suspension. The spring cannot be maintained as in the trot/canter transition, but must be cancelled and recreated. Weight must be absorbed and pushed forward. Thus, this transition promotes a strengthening of the haunches and requires increased responsiveness to the aids. There is a good reason why we first train trot/canter transitions with a young or green horse before tackling the trot/walk transitions.

During a downwards transition, it is important that the horse slows and carries the load behind. Then, it can walk freely and at any time push off into trot energetically, developing momentum.

If the transition is executed on the forehand, the horse shuffles and it takes an increased effort to motivate him back into the trot.

The seat of the rider is challenged again at this moment. Often it happens that a rider slouches during the downward transition and thus loses basic tension. This makes it impossible for the horse to step out! The feel of maintaining a certain readiness at the walk for the next task – whatever it may be – without the horse losing suppleness, can only be achieved through a sensitive coordination of the driving and restraining aids. The rubber band may never be lost during any half-halt! This transition also develops the feel of the rider for driving forward and collecting.

The trot/walk/trot/half-halt can be ridden so briefly that everything takes place within one stride. This is a very valuable collecting exercise. The rider shortens the horse, he takes up more weight on his haunches in order to reduce the momentum, at the same moment the driving aids prevail again, and the horse immediately pushes off with the hind legs and develops new momentum. This most accomplished form of a half-halt, while the horse is in motion, is a very effective training tool for the development of the horse's strength and responsiveness. To an observer, it may almost seem as if the horse halts his motion for a fraction of a second, and then continues.

Full-Halt

A full-halt is comprised of n half-halts and always brings the horse to a stop. Here n means: as many half-halts as necessary. At this point I would like to remind you what I said earlier about standing and posture, and what you have felt on your own body. Posture is never rigid, never absolutely still. Remember that when standing with your eyes closed you could constantly feel a small shifting of weight over your feet, and that standing in reality is a kind of waving around of an imaginary plumb-line. Standing totally still does not exist. The more stable the support, the less the amount of movement will be – a broad-footed stance will be quieter than a narrower stance. A horse with his four legs has a relatively stable support base. But even here small shifts of balance take place. Posture thus does not mean to stand absolutely rock still but is rather a subtle game with one's own balance. In physiotherapy, posture is defined as a checked movement, from which movement can redevelop at any given moment. This applies fully to the full halt. The horse should stop in a way that it can start off at any time into the desired movement without much effort.

For stopping, so many half-halts follow each other, and the horse is asked with driving and restraining aids in such a way, that the haunches continually take up more weight and thus slow the momentum, until no leg moves in front of the other – and the horse stops. With a young horse, the full-halt should at first be allowed to taper out, until the horse is sufficiently trained that it can execute it immediately. During the entire full-halt, just as at the halt itself, the forward tendency must be maintained. The horse should be, at any time, ready to go into new movement. Halting like this, with a constant tension of readiness to start immediately into any desired gait, is an extreme form of collection. To fine tune this basic tension between the driving and restraining aids to such a degree that the horse appears to be standing still in a seemingly very relaxed way is part of the highest art of riding. This means about five seconds of immobility: to halt the momentum for five seconds, without losing the forward tendency of the movement! If this basic tension is lost, we would have to compare, strictly speaking, between a horse just standing there and a horse at the halt!

The rider as well must maintain their posture during the full-halt. Only then can they set the horse from the halt back into motion with invisible aids. The full-halt requires from horse and rider a great deal of concentration and strength. The actual level of training of horse and rider has to be considered for this. A tired horse or a sluggish rider would be overtaxed with this demand!

A full-halt can only be as good as the preceding work. Only a horse which submits obediently to the driving and restraining aids while in motion can be checked willingly and correctly. Practising full-halts where the horse and rider have not at least mastered the rudiments of this interplay always ends up in a pulling backward – unfortunately this can be seen much too often!

Ride forward, feel the 'rubber band' and allow the horse's back to swing, and you will penetrate deeper into the secret of riding!

7.8 Inside and Outside Aids

The horse must be contained in between the lateral aids in the same measure as it is secured between the driving and restraining aids. Here as well, a proper interplay is created between the outside and inside aids. Only when inside and outside correspond with each other can the horse orient himself on the rider and be correctly positioned, bent or straightened.

When I was a child, one instructor demonstrated to me very vividly why inside without outside does not work. Once again I had pulled too much on the inside rein, and of course the horse eluded any correct flexion and bend. The instructor took my whip away and bent it between his hands and his knee in a crescent shape.

His knee was the inner leg, his hands were outside rein and outside leg. And if one hand or the knee lets go, the entire bend would be lost. Working with the inside aids without the supporting outside aids can therefore never lead to flexion, bending or straightening the horse. In addition, this picture also explains why the supporting leg is a little further back than the driving leg.

Containing

Containing a horse means to put it between all the aids in such a way that he can orient himself on his rider at any given moment during a movement. This word is mostly used in connection with the inside and outside aids since it is most obvious there. When a horse is not contained laterally, he throws the haunches to the outside in a turn, he becomes loose in front of the withers. But containing a horse is more than that. It encompasses the whole horse and his whole way of moving. The rider delimits the horse inside and outside, driving and restricting, suppling and collecting. We can say that in all dimensions of movement – front, rear and height – the rider has to 'surround' the horse. The three-dimensionality of movement is again addressed here! One could also imagine a balloon, at the centre of which are horse and rider. This balloon flies through a riding arena and as long as the rider truly contains their horse they are able to stay in this balloon. But as soon as the horse eludes the aids it leaves the circle of aids and the balloon bursts. Maybe this picture helps you to imagine better the unity of movement of horse and rider, and why some riders forget everything around themselves and cease to hear or see anything else while riding their

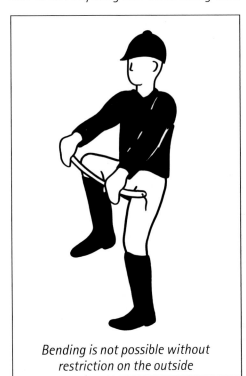

Bending is not possible without restriction on the outside

horse in deep concentration.

Flexion

Flexion takes place at the horse's poll. The definition of poll is the beginning of the neck right behind the ears. There the first cervical vertebra joins the skullcap. This joint is of extraordinary importance and function. There has to be a reason why riders are always so obsessed with riding the horse through the poll, and why even the greenest beginner soon learns that things are okay once the horse takes the head down. Some never learn the feel achieved when the haunches take over increased weight.

In a human, the head-joint is considered the first segment of movement, and in the infant movement develops from the head to the trunk and from there to the extremities. Earlier I discussed how important it is to always look into the direction of movement since the head initiates and guides the movement. Merely moving the eyes to the right can trigger a turning of the head to the right, then the shoulder girdle follows ... A rider who inclines the head to one side immediately has a different tension of readiness in their musculature. Of course, we can squint to the right while turning the head to the left – just try this. But it is a lot harder to do than moving head and eyes in the same direction.

There is no difference with the horse. Here as well, the head-joint is the first segment of movement, and the head leads the movement. When a horse is 'caught' there, the rest of the body must follow, if not inevitably, then at least reflexively – a fact which makes sensitive riding easy for an accomplished rider. At this head-joint muscles, ligaments and tendons originate which are very important for the balancing of all movement. By giving at the poll, the

long neck ligament is stretched starting from its origin and is put into light tension. Only then can the back of the horse come up and swing. Horses who elude the rider at this segment often break between the third and fourth vertebrae and are never truly supple; the 'rubber band' does not exist.

The lateral flexion of the poll is important for all balance reactions of the horse. Similar to a human, a basic tension of the musculature is created this way. Only when flexed correctly can the horse negotiate turns in good balance.

The rider can recognise correct flexion very well by looking at the crest of the neck. When you sit on top of the horse and flex it from the right to the left you will notice how the crest of the neck falls perceptibly to the other side. When the horse moves only the neck to one side, the crest itself can still point in the other direction. The horse is then *tilting* at the poll and is not honestly contained by the aids. When flexed correctly, one should always be able to glance at the horse's inside eye and nostril. Then one can be sure that the horse carries its head vertically and not tilted. Another criterion for observation of this is the ears. They should always remain at the same height. If the crest of the neck topples to the desired side, and you can glance at both the eye and the nostril, with both ears at the same height, you know that your horse is correctly flexed. Obtain this feeling on as many horses as possible. Each horse is a little bit different, and for each horse we need to find the optimal position. It is an interesting observation that many young horses to begin with are easier to position to the side where their mane falls. And even with older and well trained horses the side to which the mane falls often coincides with their preferred side.

In the riding theory we find the sentence: 'The inside rein creates the flexion, the outside rein maintains it. Then the inside rein ensures softness and responsiveness.' This sentence is another example of how a short, albeit not always easily under-standable sentence can be packed with a tremendous amount of information. It includes the entire corresponding interplay

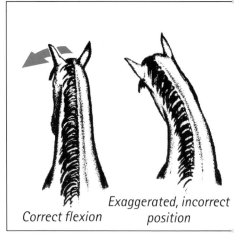

Correct flexion   *Exaggerated, incorrect position*

between the inside and outside aids. The flexion is created inside, then the horse is ridden into the outside, supporting aids so that the inside rein becomes free again and then can maintain a kind of conversation with the horse's mouth. This sounds so easy and is so difficult. When flexing the horse, the most fundamental mistakes are committed, and as a result progression of horse and rider will never be possible beyond a certain basic level.

There is no universally valid recipe for the correct flexion of all horses. Some require very few aids, others will first want to put head and neck into the desired direction, before they allow the rider to limit the flexion to the poll alone. This would equal the progress from the raw form to the fine form when learning how to move: first the large movement, which is then modified and fine tuned to the desired amount.

Horses with a thick jowl or those who tend to make themselves short and tight in this area, should initially be flexed long and low, before they can be properly flexed at the appropriate elevation. A horse, ridden long and low with its nose a little ahead of the vertical has much more space in the throat area, and, when he learns the correct flexion in this position, he will find

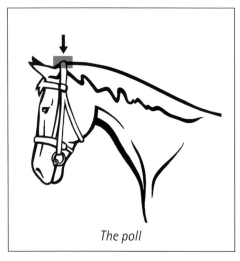

The poll

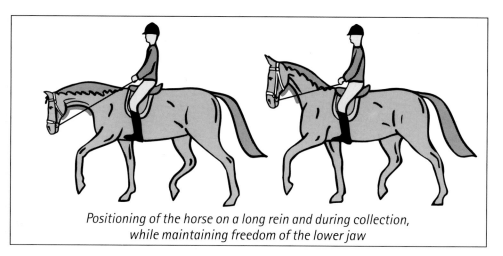

*Positioning of the horse on a long rein and during collection,
while maintaining freedom of the lower jaw*

it easier to execute flexion when then asked to do it in proper elevation, without getting tight.

The perfect fine form of a movement cannot be expected right away, either from horse or rider. But it is always important to know the aim of a movement, and to observe if one comes close to the desired end result or not. For the rider it is important to concentrate fully on the feel of *one* continuous rein. Each movement of the one hand is transmitted through the horse's mouth to the other hand. And the flexed horse is supposed to step into both reins. His whole trunk is then able to follow this beginning of movement and the horse can negotiate the turn in good balance and suppleness.

Bending

Bending is a lateral curvature of the horse's spine, as evenly as possible, from the head to the tail. The bend is limited at the trunk, because of the ribs and the sacral vertebrae. The *maximum bend* is asked for in the corners and on the volt, a lesser bend on all other curved lines. As a rule, bending is easier for the horse to one particular side. Horses and riders have their innate preference for one side or the other.

In order to bend the horse correctly, it is important for the rider to sit in good balance and influence the horse independently from his motion. The balance of the upper body is again of great importance here. I found one image very helpful in this context. When you sit on your horse, imagine that the horse's neck is your own spine. And if the neck was raised up vertically, your trunk has to be identical to the horse's neck, the horse's ears next to your ears . . .

This image can help you to follow the movement with your upper body. It is a possible way to describe the complicated way of sitting through corners. Another possibility, walking through a corner on foot, has already been described. Every lateral bending of the horse asks for rotation of the rider! This rotation in the rider's upper body has to match equally with the lateral bending of the horse.

You already have the explanation for the preferred side of your horse when riding through turns. Almost nobody possesses a perfectably symmetrical rotational ability of the spinal column. In the chapter about the upper body you learned that the main rotational centre of the spine is at the lower thoracic spine at the junction with the lumbar spine. Good control of this

'Folded back' neck of the horse

spinal segment is a *must* for every rider. After all, we cannot expect from the horse what we ourselves are unable to accomplish and dream at the same time about harmonious movement between rider and horse!

In order for the horse to remain in balance

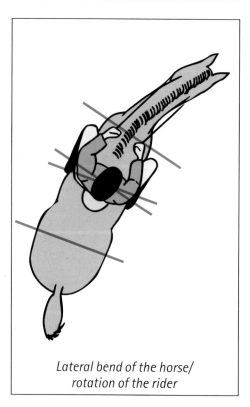

Lateral bend of the horse/ rotation of the rider

in tighter turns and at the same time to be able to step further under the weight of the rider, the *bend* is indispensable. Here as well, the rider has to make the horse at first 'hollow' with the inside aids, and then push him into the supporting outside aids in order to free the inside aids again for further influencing. This is especially the case with difficult horses.

Straightening

The forehand of the horse is adjusted to his hindquarters in a way that, when ridden on a single track, the horse learns to adapt his longitudinal axis to the line whether it is straight or curved. As a child, I learned this sentence enthusiastically by heart and impressed a good number of riding instructors and judges, without ever really having understood it.

The horse possesses a *natural crookedness* and is anatomically wider behind than in the front. Like humans, a horse has a preferred leg to stand on or to do things with. Just as a human is clearly better able to jump off from one leg, the horse pushes off with one hind leg more energetically than with the other. He prefers to step under the centre of gravity with this leg and is better able to carry weight on it. In the meantime, the other hind leg evades, preferably to the side. Thus, more weight is shifted onto the forehand. A horse who prefers to load the left hind leg, evades at the same time with the right hind and falls onto the diagonal shoulder. One can see this with an untrained horse. The different track width of front and hind legs represents another difficulty. You can observe this especially well with foals. With their long 'tooth-pick' legs, the hind legs often do not know how to navigate around the front legs. Often one can see them, with hind legs far apart, so stepping widely past their front legs on each side. Others may track with one hind leg between their front legs while the other hind leg passes on the outside. If they maintain this feature later on, they are very difficult to straighten. However, I never saw a foal that would track with both hind legs between the front legs.

One can also observe this during the training of a horse. Especially when lengthening the strides or during half-halts, young horses tend to step wide behind instead of under their centre of gravity. Only straightening work will help to get their hind legs under the centre of gravity and enable them to take over some of the load there.

Again and again one hears and reads how important the inside hind leg is. Even during the rising trot one loads the inside hind. To be found trotting on the wrong diagonal is quite disgraceful for any rider, and in young rider tests we watch like a hawk for this. When riding on the trail along a slope, one is supposed to position the horse downhill and at the rising trot to load the downhill hind leg. Why is this? If you know how to ski, I am sure you know the answer. When skiing, you always load the downhill ski, otherwise one would end up in the snow at the next turn. Loading the downhill side is therefore very important for balance during forward movement or in a turn.

This is the same when riding. The engine is located behind, and in order to achieve good balance the horse must put the downhill facing leg further underneath his centre of gravity. In the arena the downhill facing leg is synonymous with the inside leg. This is only logical since in each turn centrifugal forces are created which are directed upward and outward. Inside, a hole would be formed. This small scenario is important in order to understand why during the *straightening work* the forehand of the horse has to be aligned with the inside hind leg. The outside hind leg is then contained by the supporting outside leg of the rider and encouraged to

step underneath the centre of gravity as well.

Natural Crookedness

As you can see in the diagram, it doesn't come easily and naturally for a horse to move with a straight body along a wall. The young and unbalanced horse will try to 'support' his outside shoulder on the wall, while an older horse is apt to evade straightening work at the end of a long side by taking the hind legs to the inside onto another track. Thus, schematically speaking, straightening means to bring the horse's forehand so far to the inside that the inside hind leg follows exactly in the track of the inside front leg. The outside hind leg is brought under the centre of gravity by the rider's outside leg.

When a horse is standing on all four feet evenly, one should see, from the front, four feet, since the horse is wider behind. However, in the dressage arena, when the horses go arrow straight down the centre line and stand square at X (wouldn't this be nice!), the judge sees only two legs. Consequently, straightening work brings the hind legs closer together and more underneath the centre of gravity of rider and horse. Moving on a narrower track at the same time means a smaller support base. Standing then demands increased basic tension of the musculature. From the narrow and less stable support base, the horse can move more quickly and easily into any movement the rider desires. Therefore, the success of straightening work is especially evident in half-halts, full-halts, transitions, lengthenings . . .

An important part of *straightening* the horse is the *bending*, in order to be able to adjust the forehand to the hind-quarters. Decreasing and increasing the size of circles, serpentines, shoulder-in, haunches-in and haunches-out . . . All these exercises help to straighten the horse. The horse has to learn to accept softly and willingly the containing aids of the rider, without losing suppleness or forwardness.

The biggest and most common mistake when bending and straightening a horse is not to ride the horse forward enough. Each turn requires strength and impulsion. And when the forwardness is lost in a turn, the horse inevitably comes onto the forehand and becomes tight. Only a push-off from behind enables a horse to free his front-end and to carry himself. Only then can the rider gain influence over the forehand and position it as desired. The more weight the horse takes up behind, the lighter the forehand becomes and the easier and freer the front end can move and be adjusted to the hindquarters. Remember the famous statement: 'Ride your horse forward and make him straight!'

The rider should also straighten themself.

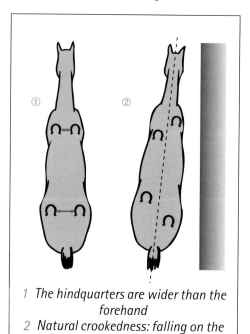

1 The hindquarters are wider than the forehand
2 Natural crookedness: falling on the outside shoulder

The entire trunk must find a harmonious balance within itself. Shoulder girdle and pelvis have to fit to each other, to the horse and to the movement at hand. This follows from the previously discussed complexity of the rotational seat, where the spine is supposed to feature a harmonious interplay of muscles in all directions of movement. Given that this is so hard for us, maybe we can give more credit to the horse because of the problems, and once again thank horses who move correctly in spite of our mistakes.

Rotation is of major importance for the straightening of the upper body. In the paragraph about bending I discussed in detail the connection between the lateral bend of the horse and the rotation of the upper body. In the development of movement in the body, rotational movement ranks at the highest level. It is the most refined movement, and only through it are sensitive balance reflexes possible. For example, when walking, this rotation is required continuously. Pelvis and shoulder girdle are connected through this rotation with a very close interplay of the muscles.

If there is a blockage anywhere in the body or not enough free movement, it is compensated for with increased movement in another place. When walking, a lack of rotation is compensated for by a lateral evasion of the hips and an altered swinging of the arms, mostly intensified from the elbows on. Riding and walking are closely related. A rider who is not straightened within themself will compensate with increased movement of their extremities. In order to compensate for the deficiencies of their basic seat, they will also have to exert much more strength when applying the aids. A one-sided unsteady hand of a rider is often caused by a limited rotational ability of the spine to one side. This realisation also leads to conclusions about the horse. Horses who

Turning at the canter

have difficulty bending or staying straight often exhibit different movement of the legs and mistakes in rhythm.

Rhythm is therefore not only a criterion for suppleness but it is also of fundamental importance during any phase of training.

Lateral Movements

Lateral movements improve the horse's flexibility and put him securely between the aids of the rider.

Leg Yielding

Leg yielding is not a true lateral movement but is a kind of preparatory exercise. By definition, it is a forward-sideways move-ment where the horse is only flexed, and remains otherwise straight within his body. The horse is flexed toward the opposite side of his movement and yields to the inside leg of the rider. Young horses learn to bring their inside hind leg underneath the centre of gravity and to submit willingly and responsively to the rider's

forward-sideways driving and supporting aids. Leg yielding allows inexperienced riders to learn the feel for coordinating the inside and outside aids. Leg yielding schools obedience to the rider's aids which are necessary for development of the lateral movements. During continuing training, the horse learns to follow the inner leg of the rider with his inside hind leg into the direction of movement and not to move away from it (as in leg yielding).

Shoulder-in

Shoulder-in is the basic lateral movement.

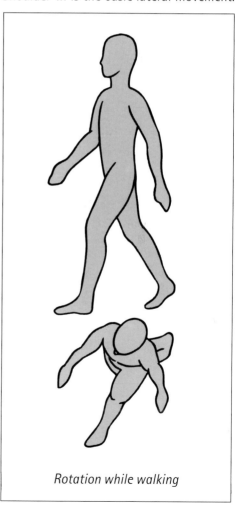

Rotation while walking

In order to achieve it, the rider asks for an increase of flexion of the horse until it moves clearly in a shoulder-fore position. The horse is then gradually asked for the necessary lateral bend which is an indispensable part of all lateral movements.

In the shoulder-in the forehand of the horse – and not just head and neck! – is taken to the inside until the inner hind leg tracks into the hoofprint of the outside front leg. For this to happen the horse must bend. Thus, the horse's inside hind leg steps directly underneath his centre of gravity, and the horse can learn to balance and carry himself optimally. It is for this reason that shoulder-in is also very helpful for other movements. Horses who try to fall in with their hind legs at the end of a long side, can easily be corrected with shoulder-in before and after the turn. Before applying half-halts and full-halts, shoulder-in offers an ideal possibility to balance the horse so that the required movement can be executed truly from the hindquarters. A horse who falls constantly onto his forehand during half-halts can carry himself better in the shoulder-in and thus shifts weight more easily to the hindquarters. Before riding a circle, one can prepare this maximum bend nicely with a shoulder-in. A spooking horse can often be ridden obediently past the problem area when in shoulder-in.

Important criteria for the shoulder-in are the bend and the simultaneous forward tendency of the horse. The most common mistakes are a lack of outside aids and over-bending the horse in the neck in front of the withers.

Haunches-in

In the haunches-in the horse is bent to such a degree that the outside hind leg follows the track of the inside front leg. Horse and rider look in the direction of movement.

Sitting correctly to the haunches-in is crossroads of riding. Here, the rotational seat is demanded to perfection. In the haunches-in, we can most clearly see the faults in the seat: some riders never learn the feel for the haunches-in, or they push the horse sideways with an increased expenditure and application of strength.

The upper body must be taken along into the direction of movement. In order to visualise this the following exercise of an experienced and competent trainer has helped me. He asked me to turn toward the horse's inside hind leg during the movement, and to keep looking at it. I am sure this was very exaggerated, but the horse suddenly moved well and I acquired the feel for the direction I had to move toward.

In the half-pass, another difficulty is that the inside hind leg needs to step forward and sideways. If the rider does not follow quickly enough with their upper body into the direction of movement they will always remain behind the motion and load the outside hind leg. In order to avoid this, rising trot in the half-pass can be helpful. Then one can clearly feel the outside hind leg hitting the ground, and this makes it easier for the rider to move at the right moment rhythmically into the right direction.

Another, a little unconventional, tip for feeling correctly balanced during a lateral movement is: 'Take off the saddle!' Without a saddle, you can feel your seat bones much more distinctly next to the horse's spine and you can clearly determine whether you are loading your inside seat bone forward-downward, or if you are collapsing in the hip and evading by using your upper body as a lever. Horses who find lateral movements difficult can often be more easily shown what is required of them without a saddle. The saddle remains an alien object between horse and rider. Of course, the saddle

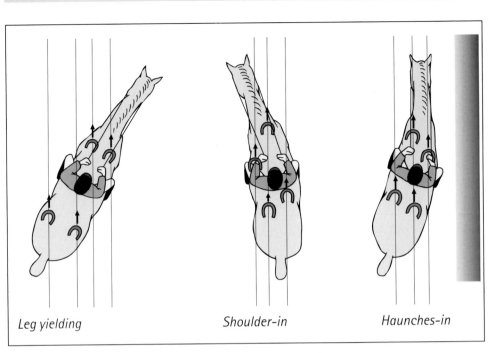

Leg yielding   *Shoulder-in*   *Haunches-in*

allows much better stability for the rider and thus facilitates a stronger influence. But many seat faults can be wonderfully concealed with a saddle, from the instructor as well as from oneself. Without a saddle, one is a lot more dependent on balance and much less able to compensate through strength.

A powerfully and forward-ridden half-pass, where the horse just seems to dance along, is to me one of the most beautiful experiences that riding has to offer.

8.

Problems – Causes – Corrections

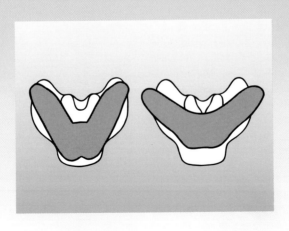

There are no tips or individual exercises for creating the perfect rider or the perfect horse. If we want to get ahead, it is important to recognise where and why some difficulties arise. Some problems are not recognised right away, but they interfere when a more subtle influencing is required. Thus, riders can learn to master the three basic gaits even in the chair seat, but they will never be able to develop quick and sensitive reactions for further influencing the horse because they are always behind the movement.

In the following, I have tried to point out the most commonly occurring problems and to offer ways to solve them. There is no universally valid recipe. But I would like to give you some ideas to encourage you to work on yourself. Even if it is toilsome it is worth it!

8.1   Balance Problems

Riding is a balance game of horse and rider. Two living beings are supposed ideally to find a common balance so that it appears to an observer as if they have grown together. The sublime, quietly sitting rider represents the ideal aesthetic picture of riding. Any layman would be able to recognise a good rider by this calm attunement. As soon as the rider's influence becomes visually distracting, disquiet rules the picture. The sensitive balance of horse and rider is at risk.

Recall again the example of standing. To stand 'still' is impossible, you are constantly balancing anew above your support base. Therefore, posture does not mean keeping still but rather balancing in its most subtle form around an imaginary plumb-line. The same applies to the *balance* when riding, in the dressage seat as well as the forward seat. Certain balance reactions are constantly taking

place and the more finely coordinated they are the more invisible they become to an observer. *Balance* is therefore not a definitive and constant condition, but a very mobile dynamic activity which repeatedly reacts and needs to be created over and over again. This activity is defined as the 'minimum of movement and tension that is necessary to maintain a stable balance'.

Theoretically, almost all riding mistakes can be classified as balance mistakes. Each riding fault leads to a disturbance of harmony, and balance can no longer be correct. Horse or rider, one or the other, is out of balance. In order to find the right realignment, it is important to recognise where and why balance is lost.

At the very moment when balance is lost, reactions occur, involuntarily and quite automatically. For example, when walking on top of a balancing beam, one starts to flail with the arms in order to compensate for a lack of balance. When riding, the arms react similarly and the legs grip tighter. If the rider loses only a minimal amount of balance, the musculature can compensate for this. Then, the rider does not fall off, but a completely independent and supple seat is not possible either – a source of many

Balanced seat

Discreet chair seat

Extreme chair seat

Discreet fork seat

*Fork seat with tense
shoulder girdle*

*The rider, sitting ahead
of the motion, disturbs
the movement of the horse*

*The horse puts the rider
into the fork seat and
comes onto the forehand*

In balance

Ahead of the motion

problems such as stiffness, crookedness, unsteady hands . . .

Some balance problems are so minimal that they are unnoticeable at the first glance. It is important to know that poor balance or a lack of it can only be compensated for by an increased expenditure of strength and counter movements.

Balance can be lost in all possible directions: to the front or back, to the side, upward (when being thrown out of the saddle) or, at the extreme, downward (when falling off). In order to better summarise various problem situations, I have divided the problems into groups. The obvious balance problems when the rider comes ahead or behind the motion are most visible when viewd from the side. The lateral deviations I will mention when

discussing the problem of crookedness/asymmetry.

Balance is always established over some kind of support base. Its centre is located there, and this is also where corrections, if necessary, have to be initiated. In the dressage seat, the support base is the triangularly shaped *seat base*. The legs stabilise the seat and the long upper body needs to be properly balanced. If the loading of the seat base is already faulty, a chain reaction of balance problems is triggered. If the seat base is loaded too far to the back, the rider is sitting on their seat bones only, resulting in the *chair seat*. When the pubic bone is loaded to a greater degree, the rider finds themself in the *fork seat*.

In balance

Ahead of the motion

Behind the motion: the young horse promptly reacts to the loss of balance and is unable to maintain the canter

The chair seat is the classical form of *coming behind the motion.* Due to this increased loading of the rear part of the seat base the pelvis is tilted backwards, the lumbar spine is rounded, the thoracic cavity collapses and the head is pushed forward as a counterweight. Equally, the arms are stretched forward, the elbow joints often get tight and the hands become extremely unsteady. The legs can no longer hang freely from the hip, they are taken more to the front and the knees have the tendency of sliding upward. The lower leg is too far out in front and the stirrup slides onto the instep.

In the fork seat, practically the opposite happens. The increased front loading of the seat base leads to a forward movement of the pelvis and an intensified hollow back at the lumbar spine. The forward-thrusted chin tries to salvage balance. The elbows frequently point backward and outward in an attempt to make up for a lack of balance in this region and the hands are pushed down. The rider is sitting on the inner thigh musculature which can no longer be released. The lower leg is taken back, and often the tip of the foot is groping for the stirrup while the ankle joint is all tense.

The length of the stirrups is a potential cause for chair seat or fork seat. In the photos on page 139, the stirrup length discrepancy is eight holes. Too short a stirrup encourages the chair seat, too long a stirrup forces the rider into the fork seat.

In the forward seat, balance problems take

Behind the motion: with an experienced horse the loss of balance is not so evident, he can maintain the canter, but loses rhythm and suppleness!

Balanced forward seat over a jump

degree, the lower legs slide too far forward and the buttocks acquire the tendency to come down again and again in the back of the saddle. These riders are not able to move their weight forward with the motion and when, for example, trotting over cavalettis, they keep falling into the horse's back since they are unable to balance their weight through knees and stirrups for some distance. Their buttocks keep pulling them backward and downward, and as a result, the hands are working backward which can restrict over a jump a necessary yielding with the hands.

even more effect. The support base is indeed wider in the forward seat, but lower, as you have read earlier. The broad support base allows for better lateral stability. To the front and rear the seat becomes decidedly less stable which is of great importance for the dynamics of increasing speed and when jumping. Also, in the forward seat one can differentiate between the two major mistakes, namely *come in front and behind the movement.*

Riders who come behind the movement often do not flex their upper body in the hip but are rather rounding their back while their pelvis remains pushed to the rear. The knees are stretched to a greater

Those riders who lean on their horses' necks like clutching monkeys are in front of the movement. The upper body is often bent forward too much and the seat bones are not pushed backward to the same degree. Owing to this, the rider's weight shifts to the front, the rider becomes unbalanced and therefore supports themself on the neck of the horse. The rider's lower legs slide back a little which makes the seat unstable, and at the smallest misstep or mishap of the horse, such a rider tumbles right off over the horse's shoulder. Instead of decreasing the load on the horse's back, this seat

The rider hangs ahead of the motion and thus causes a mistake of the front legs

A tight hand puts the rider behind the motion and disturbs the balance of the horse (evident on neck and front legs)

increases the weight of the horse's forehand which is detrimental in the long run; when riding downhill the horse will most likely be thrown off balance. When jumping the horse will find it much more difficult to lift his forehand, a frequent cause for faults with the front legs.

Balance, the secure balancing above a support base, requires much dexterity and feel for movement. Problems are most easily recognised during movement and many of them are evident at the rising trot. At the rising trot, the constant change of the support base from low and wide to high and narrow requires from the rider a great deal of coordination and balance. Here, one can already deduce minimal tendencies of the seat. If the rider, as when sitting down, plops back into the saddle, he has the tendency to come behind the motion. He has forced the rise and allows his weight, which was never really brought forward in a balanced manner, to simply flop back into the saddle.

Rising up too high and too fast, which mostly ends in a reach to the end position of the hip joints, has a hectic effect. The rider gets up faster than the horse's back comes up to meet him. This interferes with the horse's flow of movement, and in most cases he will tense the back and lose some of his natural forwardness.

From the correct rising trot, the rider can change at any time to the dressage seat or the forward seat without disturbing the horse's balance and movement. The rising trot appears effortless. Getting up and sitting down are in harmony with the lifting and lowering of the horse's back which determines the speed and the extent/height of the rider's up and down movement.

When the horse moves forward with good regularity, a slightly unbalanced seat can be hidden quite successfully. The lack of balance becomes apparent only when speed, gait or direction change. Then, the lack of basic balance manifests itself. Some typical problems, specific to the seat, develop.

The rider's 'looking down onto the horse' has a great impact on the entire balance situation. For this, refer once more to the chapter on the upper body. When you are sitting with your upper body erect, lean forward from this position and the back muscles come into play. When leaning back, the abdominal muscles are activated. Merely letting the head hang

During take-off the rider has come behind the motion – the horse cannot develop a bascule, the forelegs paddle in the air

When not disturbed in his balance, the same horse demonstrates good technique with the front legs

forward results in the back musculature working harder; a compensatory leaning back of the torso slows the reaction of the correcting abdominal muscles. In practice this means that a rider who is looking down always sits a little behind the motion and is not able to react quickly enough.

In the chair seat, the basic tension of the body is lower, the trunk is collapsed. As soon as the rider is asked to react, they first have to establish the necessary basic tension. When riding, this means that the rider often reacts too slowly, they are always 'a day late'. However, aiding the horse requires very quick reactions. Riders with a backward tendency of the upper body cannot influence the horse quickly enough. By the time their aids are given to the horse, the crucial moment is past. Often, when the crucial moment of giving the aids has been missed, the hand has a backward effect. The hand that does not give to the horse's mouth also has a backwards effect. So, the backward tendency of the upper body prevents independence of the hands – the hands most often react backwards and are pulled up in critical situations.

In the fork seat, the musculature of the rider becomes rather tight. He is cramped, often feeling unpleasant and painful. In the chair seat, some riders feel extremely comfortable because they do not have to work so hard while wobbling around on the horse's back. They do not seem to be conscious of how this backward sitting and riding affects the horse. I have never met a rider who feels comfortable and content in the fork seat. This cramped, tight seat leads to stiffness. The rider sits on the inside of their thigh muscles, the adductors. They are perched on the horse like a clothes peg and are prone to lose balance altogether and fall off at the slightest incident. Following the motion of the horse is impossible because of the extreme muscle tension. The necessary

suppleness cannot be achieved. In the transitions, the rider rams themself which, like a vicious circle, leads to more pain or at least discomfort. The rider reacts with increased cramping and becomes even less able to adjust to the motion below.

Loss of balance instantly triggers fear in the rider. Fear, consequently, leads to loss of movement with the rider reacting in a typical pattern – mostly clamping legs and backward pulling hands. The horse, too, is unbalanced by the rider's loss of balance. And the horse finds this extremely unpleasant and becomes afraid as well. The horse reacts usually by losing rhythm and suppleness. Insecure and tense, he moves stiffly through the arena. Some horses become lazy and would like to come to a halt to be on the safe side, they have no trust in an uninhibited forward motion. Others show tense strides or run uncontrollably forward.

A horse whose balance is upset several times over a jump will sooner or later not dare to take this jump. The correction which intends to re-instill confidence in the horse to once more sail freely over the fence is often wearisome and filled full of set-backs. Horses have excellent memories, they never forget experiences. One can only try to give the horse new and positive experiences which must be stronger than the previous negative experiences. Thus, a horse who was hurt quite badly at a certain type of jump will never approach this jump again totally free from concern. Here, a confident and experienced rider is needed who is able to instill in the horse enough self-confidence to overcome this insecurity before the jump. Basic talent, responsiveness and obedience play an important role.

In dressage, it is not quite as obvious as in jumping, but is just as important. A horse who has been hit hard in the back a few times during a full-halt will not maintain a supple back during the transition. Most likely he will throw up his head, stop abruptly on the fore hand . . . these are the natural consequences. When cantering on, balance is lost frequently: the horse will then leap into the canter with a high croup and head in the air. The transition loses impulsion and forwardness. These examples are meant to appeal to the rider who contributes to the cause of these faults, not to blame the stubbornness of the animal; more often than not, it is the consequence of poor and unbalanced riding. To correct this takes time, patience and maybe even a different rider, because a new level of confidence needs to be established in the horse.

Correction

How is *balance* created, how is it learned and how, when necessary, corrected?

In order to answer these questions, I would like once more to remind you of the motor development of children. Children rule over the domain of dexterity and balance. They unconsciously train their sense of balance on a daily basis during thousands of playful situations. The development of movement happens through movement to posture. Thus, infants learn the quadruped position while first wobbling and teetering, until they are able to stand up in balance. They are first able to walk before managing to stand freely . . .

A child perceives and learns a new movement complex with the whole body. An adult has to piece together a new movement laboriously from separate known movements.

An example is the rising trot, a very important balance criterion. My four-year-old niece watched me at the rising trot and declared with full conviction that she could do this, too. She had never tried it before. On the horse, she succeeded at the first try perfectly, without my giving her any instructions or corrections. Children learn movement in a complex way. Their well-formed sense of balance bestows them with great dexterity and the ability to react to new situations with their whole body. This is more difficult for the adult person. The sense of balance is no longer pronounced, the extremities have a different leverage than in children and almost always the head wants to know what kind of movement it is supposed to govern. Thus, a reflex-like reaction in the sense of a complex balance reaction is not possible. The adult has to put together a new movement piece by piece until they are able to execute it, with lots of practice, automatically. Thus, in a sense, the child does not have to practise but only needs to grasp the new movement.

Nevertheless, adults can learn and develop balance. To play a little bit of the child in the process would be an advantage. Whenever one strives for instant perfect form of balance, tension and loss of balance are often the result. Here the same rule must be applied – *from large to small – from the raw form to the fine form – through movement to posture.* When riding, specific balance training of the upper body is possible. Move your upper body in front and behind the vertical, find your own middle position as discussed in the chapters about anatomy. Erectness in the sense of length of the entire spinal column is of crucial importance!

Alternating frequently between forward seat and dressage seat with a medium stirrup length can be helpful. When at the rising trot, just remain standing in the stirrups for a few strides. Thereby you can feel yourself if you have the tendency to come in front of the motion or behind it. Patting the horse while at the rising trot, riding over cavalletti and low gymnastic jumping promote balance, reaction and dexterity.

Balance in transitions has to be trained extensively with calmness and patience. The transition from the trot to the canter seems to be the most difficult for the rider. To adjust to the changing movement below one's seat and to initiate it at the same time is not easy. For better control, you can use the small strap at the pommel of the saddle. If you succeed in putting equal forward and upward tension on the strap during the transition, you have with certainty independent hands, and this is only possible if the basic seat is in balance.

The feel of one's own body is not an objective measure. Many riders think that they are sitting straight, and only when they see themselves in a photo or video do they realise, to their horror, that they hang over backwards, that their legs are pushed out to the front ... To control our balance with the help of an instructor or a video is important for the development of a correct feel for our own balance and the ability to correct our posture when riding alone.

To sit in balance, while using a minimum of movement and strength to stabilise the seat, opens the way for a subtle and sensitive application of the aids. To ride beautifully, without using a lot of strength and leverage in the extremities, is a rewarding goal, worth working hard for – also for the sake of the horse!

8.2 Asymmetry

Everybody has their own innate *natural crookedness*. Only when viewing another from a distance could one think that we humans are built symmetrically. This asymmetry of our body is already apparent in our handedness – just try as a right-hander to brush your teeth with your left hand! Almost every one of us has a preferred leg for standing on. In its turn this one-sided standing effects one's entire trunk and way of moving. Many people have different size calves. Frequently, one boot seems too tight when putting it on, while the other one fits perfectly. Different length legs are also quite common. And now, we, with our crooked structure, hoist ourselves onto a horse and expect the horse to move straight! The horse has enough trouble with his own natural crookedness. Sometimes it complements the rider and masks their crookedness, but just as often it compounds the rider's problems who then always feels noticeably better in the one direction than in the other. Crookedness usually has its source in the trunk. The extremities try then to make up for this asymmetry. A lateral deviation of the spine can trigger different positions of the shoulders, arms and hands. On the other hand, an asymmetry of the extremities, like an injured elbow, can lead to considerable asymmetries of the whole body. To correct a problem successfully one first needs to detect the true cause of a crookedness.

Causes Found in the Trunk

Scoliosis is the technical term for a deviation of the spine from its basic position. Mostly, it is detectable as a lateral deviation with an increased arch of the ribs and more strongly developed muscles on the convex side. The C-shaped, single arch scoliosis is rare. Mostly, one can find two, three or even four curves. However, a scoliosis can be shaped to the front and back as well; then we speak of a hollow-round back, and when the spine is twisted within itself, which is the most difficult to detect, and then only through X-rays, we speak of a torsion in the spine.

Of course, all three directions can occur in combination, which is most often the case. A lateral flexion of the spine is always combined with a rotation. Therefore, the effect of a lateral scoliosis on the entire way of moving is serious. Amongst the different kinds of scoliosis, one differentiates between the fixed and firm scoliosis and the ones which can be actively compensated for through muscle strength.

Rarely, is a scoliosis truly set. The ones that can be actively compensated for are generally known under terms like 'weak posture' or 'damaged posture'. And, riding is a sport which can help to restore stability of the musculature especially for these widespread conditions. One-sided development or one-sided training of the musculature can be further cause for an asymmetry of the trunk. Extreme preference of one hand over the other or a one-sided sport (tennis) can cause a stronger muscle development on one side of the trunk, if the opposite side is not stable enough to counterbalance. A scoliosis-like deviation of the spine is the result. In most cases, however, this can be quite easily rectified.

A varying degree of lateral mobility of individual segments of the spine, especially in the region of the thoracic spine, can cause different height of the shoulder blades. Special attention should be given here to the rotational movement.

Degenerative changes, deformities of the spine after prolapsed discs or other diseases often result in loss of motion and asymmetries. In an individual case like this, a doctor (if possible, with riding knowledge!) should decide if riding is a wise sport for such a clinical picture.

Causes Found in the Extremities

Restricted mobility of one or more joints can cause crookedness of the whole body. For example, if you always hold your hands at a different height, you should test the joint mobility of your elbow and shoulder joints in comparison to each other. If you do not come up with a finding, the cause is most often located centrally in the trunk.

Musculature can be shortened, and it can be of different elasticity or strength. One-sided weaknesses of the musculature are often the reason why a rider becomes more and more crooked in the course of a riding lesson.

Injuries of all kinds are the most common cause for asymmetries connected with the extremities. Bone fractures, tenosynovitises, muscle tears are all examples.

Degenerative changes occur mostly symmetrically, but sometimes they happen only and more severely on one side. Arthritis, rheumatism are examples.

This listing of the possible causes of crookedness is not meant to encourage

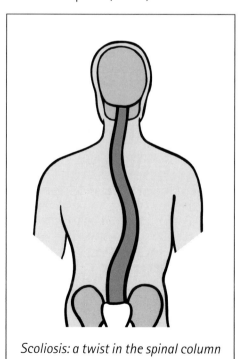

Scoliosis: a twist in the spinal column

Collapsing in the hip (from behind)

Collapsing in the waist (from behind)

Collapsing in hip and waist (from behind)

Collapsing in the hip (from the front)

Collapsing in the waist (from the front)

Collapsing in hip and waist (from the front)

you to tell your riding instructor in your next lesson: 'I can't sit straight, I have scoliosis.' On the contrary, recognising a cause is not an excuse, but an appeal to work on the real cause, and to achieve a fundamental improvement of posture and way of moving for everyday life!

When mounted, asymmetry of the trunk manifests itself more frequently in two typical posture problems: collapsing in the hip or in the waist. This happens mostly in a turn, when striking-off into the canter, in lateral movements or when applying one-sided aids the wrong way. Often the collapsing hip and waist happens together, but since cause and effect can be very different, I would like to discuss both kinds of collapsing in more detail.

Collapsing the Hip

When collapsing the hip, the base of the seat is no longer loaded correctly. You may remember that we compared the forward and downward pushing of the inside hip

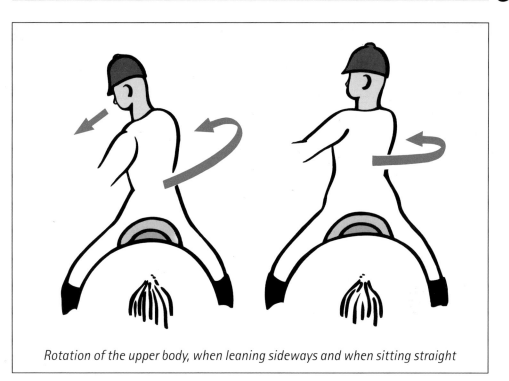

Rotation of the upper body, when leaning sideways and when sitting straight

with a tilting onto the inside base of the seat triangle, and that, as a result, all weight aids are combined with a forward movement. Especially in those moments, when this loading of the inside seat base is required, the rider must take care to remain with the forward motion. If they do not sit toward the front they will come behind the motion. Their weight stays behind and they slide to the outside.

As a result, the inside leg is turned more towards the outside, and the rider will try to grab hold with their thigh, and sometimes the lower leg. Independent aiding with the inner leg, which in turn has actually a forward driving function, is no longer possible. The outside leg usually slides uncontrollably forward in the turn and the horse is no longer contained by the rider's seat. The spine is not necessarily affected by this. Therefore, a rider with a collapsed hip can still have a fairly stable balance in the upper body.

Collapsing the Waist

This balance changes when a rider collapses in the waist. Here the evasive movement takes place directly in the spine, and usually at the junction of the thoracic spine and the lumbar spine. This lateral evasion usually occurs in situations like turning, bending, in lateral movements, when striking-off into canter ... also during the moments where the upper body has to be taken into the direction of movement, when the complicated rotational seat is required.

Collapsing the waist is an 'elegant' way of avoiding the rotational seat. The area of the junction of LS and TS is exactly the switch centre where the inclination to one side, the main direction of movement, is turned into rotation. The area between LS and TS can be tricky because here the main directions of mobility in the spine change. The TS is able to rotate, whereas because of the way the LS is built rotational

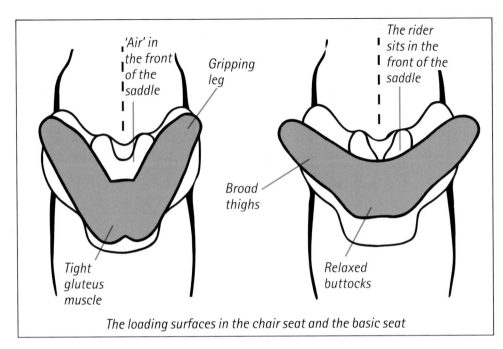

'Air' in the front of the saddle

Gripping leg

The rider sits in the front of the saddle

Broad thighs

Tight gluteus muscle

Relaxed buttocks

The loading surfaces in the chair seat and the basic seat

movements are restricted. In the TS you can rotate independently but each lateral inclination of the TS occurs in combination with a rotation to the same side. Thus, when a rider intends to ride a left turn the upper body should rotate to the left without becoming shorter. This rotation is more difficult than collapsing in the waist, where the desired rotation is achieved as well. Go ahead and try it on a stool. Turn your upper body independently by itself and then while collapsing the waist. You will feel that the independent rotation requires much more concentration.

Collapsing the waist will have a stronger impact on the upper body balance. The upper body loses tension and stability in the process. The shoulders are usually cramped and drawn up to a different height. The hands, as the last link of the series of reactions, are usually affected the most. The inside shoulder of a rider who collapses in the hip has a backward tendency, and the horse is usually pulled around the turn with the inside rein. A floppy or loose outside rein can often be observed. The horse is denied a constant connection with the rider. The weight distribution in the pelvis does not necessarily change. Thus, position of the upper and lower leg is not inevitably affected.

Most often, collapsing the hip entails collapsing the waist or vice versa as a chain reaction. The head is often held obliquely for balance reasons. To correct this problem successfully, one needs to locate the primary evasive movement. Watch yourself or a student very carefully during the most critical moments (turning, bending, lateral movements, striking-off . . .) Do they first lose control of hands and legs, do they first slide with the seat to the outside, or do they first turn the inside shoulder backward? If one succeeds in catching the problem at its root and eradicating it, then all resulting evasive movements are taken care of automatically. Especially where lateral asymmetries are concerned, correction of

In the chair seat it is especially easy to lose lateral balance

the cause is of great importance, otherwise the rider will just become more cramped and their seat more and more crooked.

When discussing the collapsing of the hip, I pointed out that the rider comes behind the motion. You need to understand the complex connection between all aspects of balance and asymmetry. The chair seat is especially susceptible to lateral deviations. When you take a closer look at the loading of the saddle you will find that a rider with a chair seat sits further back in the saddle with thighs drawn upward. Thus, a support base is created which is very stable regarding forward and backward movement but will not tolerate much lateral onslaught. This fact solves the puzzle as to why timid riders who take refuge in the chair seat fall off the side of the horse so easily in sudden turns or even just during a somewhat hectic canter transition.

The following comparison is most descriptive for the unstable form of the chair seat: 'Like a pat of butter on a hot potato!' Even if many of the old riding instructor sayings are not very flattering, the most imaginative comparison often had a justified origin!

Correction

Oh dear! One fault leads to another one, and no rider is without faults – do we dare to ride another horse with a good conscience? Do not worry, you may do so! Riding in particular is one of the few sports that requires and advances symmetry during movement. Each good movement requires a stable trunk. Thus, without a stable trunk we could neither walk nor stand. If we want to improve the way a person walks we need to discover first the cause of the problem in the trunk and then correct it. This is done almost more easily when riding than walking, for in the dressage seat the rider sits on their buttocks and movement can directly be

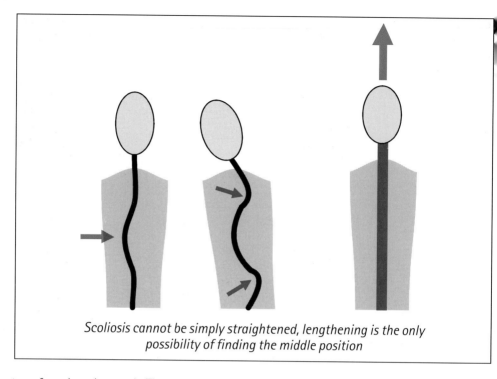

Scoliosis cannot be simply straightened, lengthening is the only possibility of finding the middle position

transferred to the trunk. The long levers of the legs are not interposed. The horse's back dictates to the rider a certain symmetry and the balancing organs are influenced to work symmetrically. This can suffice as correction for minor posture faults. Many adolescents find erect body posture enormously difficult in everyday life, but once on the horse, the motivation plus the stimuli of the horse's motion are positive impulses, and erect posture becomes much more subconscious and self-understood. It undoubtedly helps that this posture is 'posture in movement' and thus nothing rigid and cramped!

To correct an asymmetry is not quite so easy. Once you have bent a riding whip and then try to straighten it again by bending it to the opposite side, you will not succeed. The whip turns in your hand and remains obnoxiously bent as before. At the most you will succeed in creating a second arc in the opposite direction, which then makes the whip appear straight again. Our spine reacts the same way. To stretch it into the opposite direction achieves nothing, to the contrary, the crookedness or scoliosis gets rather worse.

The body holds the critical segments of the spine tight, they are moved like rigid cement blocks. Thus, counter stretching affects the segments above and below the cement block, which results in over-mobility and instability. What has to be done first is to make this block supple. Then, when the joints work freely again one can set about working on symmetry and the feel for symmetry and erectness.

And now, I am coming to a physiotherapist's favourite word: 'Length!' When you take a piece of string and lie it on the floor in curves, it is noticeably shorter than when lying straight.

The longer you protract something the straighter it becomes, or, vice versa, every deviation of the neutral (middle) position coincides with a loss of length. Consequently, if you wish to get rid of your crookedness you have to lengthen your trunk. A nice image here is the garden hose lying in curves on the lawn. As soon as the water is turned on the hose tries to straighten as much as possible due to the space-demanding water pressure. And who hasn't experienced a hose going its own way, slipping from the hand, while hosing down a horse's feet or watering the arena?

The spine reacts in a similar way. When you erect yourself from the inside out as if you are turning on a water tap in the pelvis, and you allow this erectness to reach through the entire spine all the way up to the back of the head, you can get rid of a great deal of crookedness. This feel of a long trunk should be practised extensively. It is important before each movement, when riding a transition, before each turn and in effect always and all the time. Only then can you move your upper body freely into any desired direction. But if a segmental movement block persists, you should refer to the exercises I discussed in the chapter of the upper body. Especially helpful then is segmental improvement of the rotation ability.

When riding, frequently one has to switch one's attention from the actual task. The more one notices the tendency to become crooked, the less one can remedy it. It is a vicious circle. Most important is a quick reaction from the rider as the quicker you are able to follow the motion of the horse, the less crooked you will become. Balance training, even if geared toward the front and back, can help to improve lateral stability.

The feel for the centre must be developed sensibly. Focus on your centre of movement, the pelvis, and feel the way you load the base of your seat. The proper loading is a prerequisite for any correction of the seat. Use the little leather strap when riding through a turn – the correct loading of the seat base needs to be maintained throughout. Then, you can feel for yourself whether you would rather collapse first the hip or the waist. Collapsing the hip requires correction to the position of the pelvis. Collapsing the waist calls for improvement of the erectness and rotation of the spine.

Of course, the horse can push the rider to the outside as it tries to avoid stepping correctly under the centre of gravity. With some horses, the saddle slides to one side and wears down there quicker if not properly taken care of. Having the panels evenly stuffed would be the first thing to do. In order to avoid being shifted to the outside, a great deal of feel and upper body balance is required. Sometimes it helps to step down firmly into the opposite stirrup. Once, during a lesson, when all of us slid to the outside in the canter, our riding instructor even offered £5.00 to the rider who succeeded in breaking the inside stirrup leather. This is surely extreme, but it made it obvious to us how much more weight we had put on the outside stirrup.

What is required is to shift the weight consistently and simultaneously together with the entire upper body into the desired direction, and not to just lean to the inside. Horses who cause their riders to sit extremely crookedly have problems with their own crookedness. Depending on talent and level of training of the horse a suitable correction has to be devised. Improving the impulsion during straightening exercises can bring about obvious changes. There is a well known saying: 'The horse should become more beautiful in his work!' And this doesn't refer only to the musculature of the horse but also to his movement. And a horse that moves in a

8.

Head bent sideways looking down

Looking down as seen from behind

Shoulder high on one side (from the front)

Shoulder high on one side (from behind)

Sliding to the outside in a turn

crooked and unbalanced way cannot be called beautiful, even if he seems to be taken from a painting when standing still.

Length applies to the horse as well. You will never be able to straighten the horse if you only try to bend him the other way. To lunge a horse more on the one side, seemingly beneficial to remedy the crookedness, is wishful thinking and ends up to be a false conclusion. Equally fatal is to make the horse tight and short or to ride it backward. One needs to encourage length in order to obtain a straight horse. Here the forward stretching of the rubber band becomes of importance again. The means of choice is a correct stretching of the horse forward and downward. At first, you should ask for turns and bending only for short periods of time, so that the horse is given the chance to develop slowly. Under no circumstance must it learn to evade by becoming short and tight.

Cheer up! You will succeed and will sit on a horse in good balance. The feeling you will then experience will reward you for the many sudorific hours it took you to get there.

8.3 Stiffness

To be stiff means not to be able to execute a desired or required movement. But riding is movement! Good riders always follow the motion with a supple seat, they are part of the horse's movement. Each time the rider fails to follow the motion, disharmony erupts and disturbs the movements of rider and horse simultaneously. Stiffness has many causes and often occurs in combination with other problems like balance.

Causes of Stiffness

Recognising the cause is the most important prerequisite for reducing stiffness. There are many reasons for stiffness. Often a so called 'vicious circle' develops, many small problems bring others about and a huge problem takes shape, often unsurmountable without outside help. The following list of causes is meant to demonstrate just how wide-ranging the phenomenon of stiffness is.

a) Joints

Joint-end Positions
If a joint is extended all the way to the end of its range of movement it can no longer be springy, there is no more play. As I pointed out in the chapter about physiology, a joint at its end position is under the tension of the capsule-ligament-apparatus. The functional middle position of a joint, as required of most joints when riding, is the position with the least pressure within the joint. It is obvious that from this position movement in all directions is possible with a minimal expenditure of strength.

Functional Disturbances/Blockages
A joint can jam just like a drawer. Then it no longer has its normal range of motion – an apparent middle position can turn into an end position. The cause for this must be explored by a specialist doctor or physiotherapist. Using the hip as an example I would like to demonstrate such causes.

You are sitting on your horse and are supposed to take your thigh further back. You either cannot do it at all or only when evading into an exaggerated hollow back in your LS. Your hip extension is limited. The consequence: a stretched dressage seat is not possible with a loose hip joint. But the cause has not become clear. Is it

shortened muscles, tendons, capsule-ligament-apparatus, too much or too little synovial fluid, cartilage damage (arthrosis)? This is not supposed to turn into an excuse for not properly stretching the dressage seat but is rather an appeal to do something about the causes of the impaired hip movement.

b) Musculature

Disturbance of the Interplay of the Muscles
Earlier, while discussing the physiology of the muscles, I explained how the musculature works. We can never scrutinise one muscle by itself, it is always fitted into a chain of muscles and works together with its antagonists in utmost synchronisation. Posture itself already influences the amount of tension present in the musculature. Thus, we also have to regard the musculature in connection with the joint position. The trunk plays a very important role in this; correct erection of the trunk is the prerequisite for any type of controlled movement of the extremities.

Weaknesses
In a muscle stressed beyond its strength, there is often a reaction of a permanent contraction which is mostly painful. A typical example of this is the tensed-up nape of the neck. Since the thoracic cavity does not carry the shoulder girdle, the entire weight of the arms is suspended from the nape and its muscle cords tense up and can hurt quite severely.

Too Much of a Good Thing
When expending too much strength and effort, for example while pushing the horse forward, muscles are stressed too much and too one-sidedly, resulting in stiff legs and/or other body segments. One then presses the lower legs so firmly against the horse that one's hips become locked and one can no longer follow smoothly the motion of the horse. Here the cause can

usually be found in an unbalanced application of the aids. In our example, the leg aids prevail. However, the entire rider from head to toe should take part in pushing the horse.

Posture, joint position, a different amount of strength or elasticity – all these are causes for an impaired interplay of the muscles. For an accurate diagnosis, we would once again need a specialist. However, not every problem immediately requires the help of an orthopaedist or physiotherapist; our own body is the best therapist. Try a number of the suggestions offered and feel how your body reacts to them. This is the best guarantee for success!

c) Respiration

The influence of respiration on our way of moving should not be underestimated. Generally, one can observe that breathing out has a relaxing effect. Quick, hectic, reflex-like inhaling raises the basic tension of the body musculature. Breathing is not dependent on the conscious mind. It is a good thing, too, that our head is free for other things and that we don't have to think about every single breath. But, on the other hand, many problems happen subconsciously: holding one's breath, irregular inhaling and exhaling in difficult situations etc. Again and again observe your breathing. It is advantageous if exhaling takes longer than inhaling and no effort is necessary for inhaling. Some conscious breathing in between can work wonders. But breathing should not be governed deliberately, we should let it happen, just like we shouldn't move on the horse but should allow ourselves to be moved.

d) Fear

Fear causes movement to become tense and is an enemy to any movement. A defensive reflex always triggers the bending pattern, an extreme case of which curls us into the foetal position. Here we have to proceed with lots of patience; fear can neither be explained nor removed rationally. The two most important ways to diminish fear are habit and distraction. Habit, on the one hand, affords secure grounding through it's repetitious routine in the work schedule (easy at first!) and delimits, for the time being, new and fear-ridden tasks. Distraction is not so easily achieved with adults as with children but just as necessary. It can be accomplished by diverting the mind through the introduction of play or through concentration on group dynamic elements (quadrille etc).

e) Stress

Stress always triggers automatisms. Depending on type, this can also be a cause for stiffness with some riders. In riding, stress can arise due to over-strain or performance pressure. However, we can create stress from somewhere else altogether, and on those days riding often does not turn out well. To have our head always free of other things so that we can fully concentrate on riding – wouldn't that be nice!

f) Coldness

A cold muscle cannot perform. In a cold joint, the synovial fluid is not the right consistency to allow for optimal gliding of the joint surfaces. When cold, we get tense, pull up the shoulders . . . The core of the body must protect the vital organs. Thus, when we are cold, the body warmth concentrates on the trunk and the circulation in the extremities gets reduced to a minimum. Even actions like rubbing the hands, breathing on them, slapping them, sitting on them or hiding them under the horse's mane cannot evoke a permanent improvement of the blood circulation.

True, riding is supposed to make us warm, but often we get onto the horse cold, doing neither of us a favour. We cannot get warm, (and by warm I mean all the way into the tips of our fingers and toes), until the core of the body is heated sufficiently so that it can afford to redistribute warmth. I have tried many so called warm-up programmes, since I have had to stand often in an ice cold indoor arena, or, on the trail, have had a few kilometres to go ... the only thing that really works is, in my experience, running. To dismount and to do a few rounds in the indoor arena with the horse in hand is the best method of warming up quickly and lastingly. Every horse is grateful to the rider who gets on with a warmed-up body.

g) Age/General State of Training

Riding is one of the few sports we can practise into old age. But, just the same, a seventeen-year-old rider will certainly be more elastic than a seventy-year-old. The latter, on the other hand, has more experience and feel which can make up for a lot of physical deficits. Again, the warm-up and suppling phase play an important role for rider and horse.

h) The Matching of Horse and Rider

Riding takes two. Therefore, when looking for the cause of a stiffness, we must consider the horse as well.

Way of Moving
Some riders cannot sit a horse with a lot of bounce, others need exactly this motion as a stimulus for their hip joints to become supple through lots of movement from below. These riders cannot sit a horse with a flat back motion and feel uncomfortable on such a horse. Each person has their own individual body oscillations and sometimes the horse just fits them. Of course, a good rider should learn to adjust to the various ways a horse moves, but it is important to consider this point when choosing a horse, whether for purchase or for a lesson. Changing the horse can sometimes solve a seat problem.

Width
The wider the horse, the further riders must be able to spread their legs in the hip joints. In the process it can easily happen that the hip joints get to their maximum spread – into an end position of movement – and they are therefore unable to follow the motion that the horse requires. On the other hand, it can prove difficult to close one's legs around an extremely narrow horse, which in turn often leads to stiffness of the legs and hips. This problem is very rarely caused by poor nourishment of the horse but is mostly an anatomical factor of the horse's trunk. Little can be done about this. A thorough consideration when choosing a saddle may be more helpful than anything.

Suppleness of the Horse
All along, I have been searching for the causes of stiffness in the rider. This is often enough the case, but the alternative may be true as well. It would be absurd to imagine a horse to be always supple, responsive and eager to work. Horses, too, have their preferred sides, and suppleness is one of the first goals of the training scale of the horse. A tense horse with a tight back and stiff, short strides will make it nearly impossible for the rider to have a supple seat. The harmony of non-restricted movement is required from the horse as well as from the rider.

Correction

'Don't get tense, loosen your shoulders! . . .' Directions like these are useless corrections since they cannot be realised. Rather the rider becomes frustrated not knowing how, where and what to let go, and the instructor becomes frustrated thinking that the student does not do as told.

There is no universal recipe for reducing stiffness. With the following pointers, I would like to outline ways to deal with stiffness and the aspects to be considered in the process. In order to find the cause of stiffness, we need to know where to look for it. First of all, we should always check the base of the seat. Even minimal balance problems in this area can have extreme implications on the suppleness of the rider. If the base of the seat is not correct, any other correction cannot be carried out. Any attempt to do so may even worsen the current condition. It is useless to repair a tower where the structure of the base is obsolete.

Also, check the position of the pelvis, look at the line of A.S.I.S. and pubic bone, observe the hip joint: do you see any movement there? Stiffness of the trunk is often combined with fidgety and uncontrolled extremities. To start the correction with the extremities would only worsen the situation. The horse's back is moving. If this motion cannot be absorbed and cushioned in the hip joints it travels up into the trunk. Imagine a row of balls, and that you knock the last ball on one end: the ball on the opposite end will bounce off. It is the same when riding: if the hip is tight, the impulse continues on and the motion may arrive at the shoulder girdle, the head etc.

The locked hip joint prevents a deep seat at the trot – the horse comes on the forehand

At the canter, the rider evades the motion of the horse with a stiff hip joint, which in the extreme can lead to . . .

. . . leverage movements of upper body against lower body and thus to an extremely unsteady seat

Unsteady hands are caused mostly by an unbalanced seat. The hands cannot be carried independently of the horse's motion. In this case, requesting that the hands be held still is wrong. It would be paradoxical. The horse is moving, and the rider should be still? On the contrary, she must follow the motion in order to conquer stiffness. In reality, the hands are not supposed to be held still but should constitute a constant connection to the horse's mouth, which in turn is supposed to be as quiet as possible. This explains why riders on the lunge line, who are asked to carry their hands quietly without holding the reins (one of the favourite seat exercises) find it difficult to hold their hands quiet when the connection with the horse's mouth is missing. It is important to always bear in mind that all joints have to participate in a movement when riding and that, when one joint is held tight, motion arrives in another joint with double force and leads there to unsteadiness and evasive manoeuvres.

Therefore, the rider has to find the joint which does not participate in the movement and work on it. Just like with a horse, the correction has to happen in a forward direction, into the movement.

The goal, which is a quiet and elastic seat, requires a coordinated interplay of the muscles and minimal movement of the joints. Again, we can well compare this with standing. Stand upright, distribute your weight evenly over both legs, (do not straighten the knees excessively!) and close your eyes. Then you can feel that you are not actually standing still but that your weight is always swaying a little above your feet. You have to readjust your balance on a continuous basis. This happens automatically and with minimal movement due to a perfectly coordinated interplay of your muscles.

How to learn this? Keep observing children, they show us the most natural way of learning a movement. A child who has just learned to walk, can walk but not stand still; when standing she wobbles and is insecure. Our muscles find movement easier than regulating balance at a standstill. Therefore, in the evolution, movement comes first, then posture, while posture is to be understood as a minimal movement!

Therefore, any riding student would be overtaxed if a quiet posture was required right at the start of their riding training. To keep still causes stiffness. Rather, we should practise movement in order to improve posture. What are the possibilities when riding? We want to improve the balance of our upper bodies above our pelvis, which is to a large extent responsible for the position of our legs. Frequent transitions from dressage seat to forward seat develop balance. Emphasised movement of the hip joints such as rising trot, also without stirrups, can remedy a locking of the hip joints. Rising trot without stirrups requires more movement in the hip joints than sitting to the trot. Again we have the opportunity to improve small movement through larger movement. When rising to the trot without stirrups, it is important to keep in mind that it does not matter how high the rise out of the saddle (which would only be done by clenching with the legs), but rather how well the hip joints follow the motion of the horse. Increasing and decreasing the tempo while taking the upper body along into the motion, or, another change, like forward seat while increasing, dressage seat while decreasing the tempo trains control of speed and rhythm which are further requirements responsible for balance and stiffness problems. Dictating the rhythm, through use of cavalletti, for example, can be very helpful. Riding on trails furthers inner and outer suppleness. Considerations on how

The horse moving with total suppleness . . .

to solve stiffness problems are a good basic concept for a riding lesson, and, by the way, laughing is permitted as well.

One should plan exactly how to design the warm-up phase. It must be appropriate for the individual needs of horse and rider. Again and again, one sees how a horse is warmed up, and much is talked about it, but the rider should not mount before being warmed up as well. I have heard lectures where a gym next to the riding arena was suggested, and in addition, an automatic walker for the horses, so that the rider, well warmed-up from the gym, can mount the already warmed-up horse.

For me, however, the warm-up phase has tremendous appeal, as horse and rider find each other in movement and application of the aids. When having the possibility to ride several horses in a row, we will observe that we ride the second horse usually better than the first since our body is already warmed up, but the riding of the third or fourth, depending on

physical condition, gets worse again because concentration and strength start to fade.

To begin with, it is important to find out where one's own individual problems of suppleness are located. In cold weather it is helpful to trot the horse in hand several times around the arena before mounting. Also, include in your warm-up work exercises for yourself. For example, practise the transition from the dressage seat to the forward seat without hampering the horse in his movement. Here I recommend shortening the stirrups slightly (one to two holes) otherwise it is easy to end up in the fork seat. Rise to the trot and concentrate entirely on the elastic downward stretch of your legs in the sitting phase in order to supple your hips. Control your hands, etc. In order to not evade by standing in the stirrups, and to get deeper into the saddle, I would recommend holding on to the pommel strap. This allows you to pull yourself down

. . . loses his impulsion and 'falls apart' when the rider is sitting too loosely . . .

The rider's locked hip causes a hollow back, high hands and pulled up knees and lower leg. The horse holds his back tight, the hind leg cannot step under and the jaws become tight

Slouched, 'slack' rider

into the saddle. By consistently loading the base of the seat you are better able to relax the hip musculature. When riding without stirrups, the weight of the legs contributes to the stretch.

Often I observe that horses warm up and let go much easier when the rider does the same! Of course, there may be a situation where horse and rider need a different warm-up programme. In such a case, we need to try different things like lungeing, free-lungeing, free-jumping etc. If both horse and rider cannot warm up and relax sufficiently, all further work is greatly impaired. Do yourself and your horse a favour, get to know yourself and all your problems, and find your way to warm up

and relax. Then there should be no limits to your future work!

8.4 Slackness

Failing to fully control only one or two joints is all that is needed to unbalance the entire seat. Too much movement develops and too little basic tension is present in the seat. This results in a much coarser and much less differentiated influence. There are many causes for slackness, and often several causes appear at the same time.

Causes for Slackness

a) Hyper-mobile Joints

For different reasons, joints can have a greater range of motion than is necessarily beneficial. This may be due to heredity or to over-stretching or tearing of ligaments. Often, such a hyper-mobile joint can no longer be enveloped properly by the musculature and is therefore often unstable. Especially in the case of a loose capsule-ligament-apparatus of a joint, proper muscular training is the only possibility to restore stability.

b) Low Basic Tension of the Musculature

Each person possesses their own individual basic body tension. There are people with a rather high and firm basic tonus of the musculature, and others who are quite slack, because their musculature has a low basic tension. This is also determined by body type.

High or low blood pressure can play a role in this. People with low blood pressure often feel lethargic and are a little limp throughout their bodies. If the whole organism is rather slack, it is difficult to keep the trunk erect. The thoracic cavity sinks down, the person collapses. As a result, breathing is restricted, metabolism is slowed down even more, a vicious circle takes its course.

c) Weaknesses of the Musculature

When a muscle lacks the strength to secure a joint, undesirable wobbly movements are the result. In such a case, the rider tries to save whatever they can and cramps visibly in the process until stiffness occurs. Observe yourself and other riders – often you can feel or observe a wobble before stiffness occurs.

The muscles to be utilised to secure a joint are the ones which slow down the motion; without this function, controlled movements are not possible. For example, if you reach purposefully for a certain object, the slowing musculature works in a very fast and precise interplay together with the leading musculature. Only then can you stop your hand precisely at the object. If this could not be accomplished, the hand would bump into the object, thus displacing it rather than gripping it. I have discussed this slowing muscle work several times as work-into-lengthening. It is the most difficult and fatiguing kind of work for a muscle, and it requires the most strength and a great deal of coordination. To stabilise dynamically not only one joint during movement, but all of them, requires from the rider lots of concentration, coordination and a good basic physical condition. This is the reason we get sore muscles so quickly when riding!

d) Balance Problem

A person fighting with balance on the horse's back, often requires more scope of their own movement at the beginning. If the upper body comes behind the motion, the leg wobbles away to the front and vice versa. Or, until a stable and balanced tower of pelvis, thoracic cavity and head is built in the upper body, wobbling can happen within the trunk. This is again closely connected with a harmonious interplay of the muscles.

e) Stiffness in other Body Segments

The human body is a unit. And, if there is too much of one thing in one place, then there is too little of it somewhere else. Thus, a kind of inner energy re-distribution is created. Applied to riding, this means that, when a rider has tightness on one end, it manifests itself as a wobble movement in a totally different location of the body. A classical example, is the wobbling head. The command to 'keep the head still', cannot be complied with, or only for a very short period of time, by cramping any number of muscles. The underlying cause of this problem can often be found in a tight hip in conjunction with a locked lumbar spine. As soon as the rider learns to let go there, elastically following the motion, the wobbly head will correct itself on its own. When slackness and wobbling of body segments occur, we should always search for the true cause. Before suggesting a correction which tries to stabilise the wobbling spot, we first have to search for the stiff regions to improve the mobility there. Movement comes before posture!

f) Wrong Comprehension and Feel of Suppleness

Many riders mean well in believing that they are riding softly and sensitively when not applying any strength. This is well and good. It is true that the more correctly a rider is sitting and the more correctly a horse is trained the less strength is necessary. But the assumption that riding can be accomplished without any strength, and especially without the proper tension, is a fairy tale. How is a horse able to develop powerful movement and dance under such a slack rider?

The rider's own erectness and collection is required for supporting the horse. Even an affectionate 'looking down onto the horse' which can be observed with many riders when concentrating on their work, inhibits the erection of the trunk and slows the responsiveness of the upper body. The impact that a drooping head has on the musculature of the trunk has been thoroughly discussed in the chapter about the upper body.

Suppleness has nothing to do with looseness or slackness. On the contrary – as explained earlier – suppleness is the basic tension of the musculature, adequate to the situation at hand, where a constant change between tensing and releasing takes place. Suppleness is a pulsating and fascinating thing which is very much consistent with a high degree of tone in the musculature. Equally, the horse should remain relaxed and supple even when asked to perform at the highest degree of collection, like in piaffe and passage.

g) Fatigue and Difficulty to Concentrate

When riding in the evening, after work and being tired, the rider can easily become too loose. Everybody has their own posture type and individual pattern of posture and movement. When tired, we are, so to speak, hanging in the joints, the musculature is no longer (or at least insufficiently) supporting them. When riding, we are moved by the horse and have to react to this movement. If the musculature cannot parry these motion impulses they run as wobbly movements through the entire body. This can be experienced well at the walk. If you fully collapse your body at the walk you will notice that the motion of the horse's back is amplified throughout your entire spine. Only after erecting your trunk will your seat appear quiet once again. No rider is without posture problems. And, some body segments are almost always more mobile than others. When the rider is tired, this area can no longer be properly secured, and evasive manoeuvres become evident.

Concentration is an important attribute for the rider. If no longer able to concentrate on a required task or a certain situation, riders evade with their own evasive movements. This can frequently end up in a too loose seat. The horse demands the entire rider with their full concentration.

h) Insecurity

Insecurity and fear always go reflexively hand in hand with the loss of erect posture. When riders are not sure of what they are doing they will not be able to ride 'erectly and proudly through the countryside'. The basic tension of the musculature is reduced as a result and the rider slides into evasive movements. Posture cannot be maintained. Fear usually brings about cramping and stiffness; insecurity often results in a loose and wobbly seat.

i) Matching of Horse and Rider

Way of Moving
No basic rules exist for this. Some riders find horses with lots of natural impulsion very pleasant. To them, this impulsion transmits impulses which advance erectness, it makes it easier for them to sit up straight and to create a good posture with the necessary basic tension. These riders are not challenged sufficiently on a horse with *flat gaits* and often evade with unstable wobbling.

Other riders are overtaxed by a lot of impulsion, and this strong movement permeates their whole body and moves individual joints or body segments without the rider being able to gain control over them. Trying out as many horses as possible can help you to find your own individual preference for a horse's way of going. At the same time, you learn to adjust to the many different ways of moving which distinguish a good rider.

Suppleness of the Horse
The warm-up phase is meant to achieve the correct suppleness of rider and horse. This does not mean that the basic tension of the musculature should be lowered, but that a sensitive interplay of the muscles should be stimulated and promoted. No muscle should remain in constant tension. It happens much too often during the warm-up phase that the rider induces too low a basic tension in the horse, recognisable by his dragging hind legs and drooping head. The rider does not fare much better in the process. One instructor once hit the nail on the head: 'You try to get your horse loose, more loose and more loose until you have lost!'

Correction

In order to correct successfully a too-loose seat, it is very important to recognise the cause of it. Otherwise there is the danger of the loosely sitting rider becoming tight and stiff!

Once again, the same rule applies: *through movement to posture.* In order to be able to maintain posture, you first need to work on controlled movement. Both too stiff a seat and too loose a seat need to be corrected through forward movement – just like a horse. To build up and experience any kind of tension at the halt is rarely beneficial. The erectness of the trunk is organised musculature which submits subconsciously and only to a limited degree to the voluntary response system. Correct suppleness orients to the situation at hand, in this case the movement of the horse. We can assume, feel and train the basic tension for the collected trot only at the collected trot.

Our own *body perception* needs to be developed. It is necessary to feel where we tend to evade and how and where we have slid into too loose a seat. We can often observe with ourselves how our upper body and seat move against each other. These movements usually meet each other in a hyper-mobile section of the spine. It can happen toward the rear through a collapsing of the thoracic cavity, and also to the front through a forward tilting of the pelvis, often resulting in a hollow back. A wobbling-toward-the-rear brings the rider behind the motion; but it is easier to correct. At the walk, for example, we can lay a hand on our sternum and create the stable-mobile feeling – stable thoracic cavity and mobile pelvis following the motion of the horse. In the process, we need to work harder with the front muscle chain, the abdominal muscles. The entire thoracic cavity needs to be taken to the front and into the movement.

The second version, evading into a hollow back, is more difficult to correct. The rider lacks a stable seat base, the pelvis evades the horse's motion to the front, so they sit in front of the motion with a tendency toward the fork seat. The deep back musculature frequently lacks the ability to lengthen and thus fails to offer support. The lower abdominal muscles are often slack and do not afford active counter support. In this case, the rider needs to work on a consistent loading of the triangular seat base. An enclosing seat, and with it a sensitive influencing of the horse, is impossible if the rider evades through wobbly movements. Priority needs to be given here to the development of the seat instead of influence. Otherwise, the rider acquires a wrong feel for the application of the aids.

Classic examples of loose seats are adolescents during puberty. During the growth spurts, bones grow faster than muscles. This leads to an uncoordinated and often lanky motion image. Fine coordination is only achieved when the body has finished growing. When riding, this becomes obvious in exaggerated and too large movements. During this phase, the musculature is not capable of assuming the basic tension that is required for fine coordination. If the instructor, for the duration of an hour, asks just that from a student, the result is usually frustration, stiffness and painful fatigue of the musculature. Nevertheless, even with such a young rider, one can sometimes glimpse and anticipate for a few moments, future development. I remember a young girl who

Circling of the arms while following with the eyes

rode quite nicely before the growth spurts set in, but once she started growing she lost coordination and started to wobble terribly even at the rising trot. Nevertheless, for a few steps and strides, she was able to place her legs in a superior manner. One could imagine what she would look like once able to ride well. Patience is all that was needed. In the meantime, in the course of two years, this young woman developed into a talented rider whose strengths are a quiet, closed and independent seat.

With this example, I would like to demonstrate that erectness and control of the body are a *maturation process* which needs to be installed into the subconscious. This takes patience and long, intensive training. A loose seat cannot be remedied from one second to the other. It must be worked on over a long period of time.

Developing the seat has priority over influence training. Use the little strap on the saddle. Pulling yourself down helps to stabilise your upper body and to load consistently the base of your seat.

Collection of horse and rider can only be assumed for short periods of time. Sit to the trot for maybe once around the arena, and when you start wobbling, go back to the rising trot and try again a little later. Increase these intervals carefully. Just as a horse becomes tense at some point when continuously ridden in collection, the same happens to the rider. When riding a horse at a high degree of collection, we must ride him forward in between, lengthening the stride or allowing him to stretch forward downward in order to preserve the suppleness of the musculature. The same applies to the rider. After a phase that requires a lot of stability of the trunk we should be able to relax again. Taking a break at the walk, changing into rising trot, lengthening the strides in the forward seat, are possible ways to reduce the high basic tension of the collected dressage seat and to give the musculature a chance of maintaining suppleness.

Unsteady hands and head, as well as wobbly legs, originate usually from the trunk. When correcting locally, we must be very careful not to produce the opposite, namely stiffness. There are some helpful exercises.

A wobbly head can be steadied successfully with the help of our eyes. Prescribing a circle with the arm and following the hand with the eyes as the arm moves in front of us quickly ends the wobbling of the head. Equally, it usually stops when we look to one side fixing our eyes upon a certain spot or object.

Unsteady hands can usually be remedied with the little leather strap, we can control ourselves as we are able to notice if we maintain an even pressure. At the same time we stabilise the trunk – the prerequisite for independent hands. Unsteady hands are especially obvious at the rising trot, when the hands are taken up while rising and lowered when sitting down. In this case, we should not try to hold the hands absolutely still; this would be substituting one extreme with the other. But it helps to try to feel the horse's mouth, to concentrate on an even contact, to adjust the hands to the horse's mouth, independent of the seat.

Wobbly legs are usually the result of overtaxing the trunk. One can observe this with an adolescent during puberty. I myself carried for a whole the nickname: 'Miss Sloppy Leg'. It helps to ride once in a while in jodhpur boots since we can feel the horse's body much better without long boots. Only when we are able to feel distinctly a certain area of our body can we work on controlling it.

Altogether, a loose seat is easier to correct than a stiff seat; carefully measured training without overwork and a little feel for motion are necessary.

8.5 Pain

The perfect rider does not exist. You have understood this by reading this book. It is not just constitutional problems or posture weakness that can be of hindrance to riding, but we are also not always fully fit when mounting a horse. And when our body aches in one place or another, a whole chain reaction of evasive movements is triggered. When our large toe hurts, we will immediately assume a different way of walking and try to avoid putting weight onto this toe. Due to this avoidance, a limp mechanism is triggered which in its turn affects, of course, the other joints like knee, hip and, in continuation, the spine. The same applies to riding. A small ache somewhere in our body can be responsible for evasive manoeuvres which do not allow a balanced and supple seat.

Of course, I could say that such a rider has no right to be on a horse, but in practice, we cannot regiment this quite so easily. For example, you come into the yard with a touch of flu and a headache. Since you do not feel well, you intend to lunge your horse. But the indoor school is chock full, it is dark outside, the outside maneges are under water, the pastures are closed or none even exist... Since you need to exercise your horse, and you cannot find another good rider who would have time to do it for you, you have to do it.

Situations like these are quite common. And sometimes you dismount after such a session having had the most wonderful ride, and pain and indisposition seem to be gone as if by magic. Clearly, riding is of major health promoting value. How many people get a handle on their back pain through riding! Therefore, generally one should not disallow riding when in pain, but should offer support as how to deal with such a pain in order to bother the horse as little as possible, and, at the same time, achieve a lessening of the pain.

However, when pain is too severe, or does not seem to let up at all, we should deliberate, for the sake of our horse, whether we should ride.

Headache

The causes for headaches are many. If they are caused by diminished blood circulation, riding can be helpful. Riding is not advisable when the pressure in the head is so high that our head seems to burst at every stride we sit to the trot. In no way can we expect improvement by continuing to sit to the trot. When we have a headache, we should avoid exertion, collection and jolts like sitting to the trot, jumping ... If you mount your horse with a headache, you have to adjust your concept accordingly. You will not want to or be able

to start an argument with your horse. You should stick to a warm-up programme that is easy on you and is one that your horse enjoys. Headaches are sometimes caused by tense muscles. Once you warm up together with your horse, you stand a good chance of dissolving your headaches.

Backache

Who has not had it? At some time or other, everyone suffers from it. If the discomfort is severe and sustained, an expert should be consulted to look for the underlying cause. With minor complaints, light cramps, small blockages, minimal strains, riding can be very helpful. The motion of the horse at the walk is especially suitable to relieve tension and tightness. At the trot and canter, the musculature is encouraged to interplay properly through impulses from below. As a result, posture improves and pain diminishes. The principle applies: 'Our own body is the best therapist!' You have to learn to listen within yourself and feel what is good for your back, what movements are helpful and what actions make the discomfort worse. Using this premise, you may ride when you like.

Stretching exercises like putting both arms around the horse's neck and slowly erecting your spine, vertebra by vertebra, patting the horse etc., can help to relax the musculature and to open locked joints.

Hip Pain

As soon as the hip hurts, we cannot keep it supple. This can be caused by limited mobility, shortened and tight inner thigh musculature, or by degenerative changes of the joint itself. If the problem is muscular, it will improve in the course of the session. You may have to ride with shorter stirrups to begin with, and only after thoroughly warming up be able to loosen and stretch your hip joints and lengthen your stirrups. Riding without stirrups, while consistently and quietly loading the seat base, can be very helpful. Other possibilities to achieve harmonious and sensitive following of the motion through larger movements are alternating between rising trot and sitting trot, changing between leaning forward and sitting upright. If the hip joint itself is affected, it depends very much on type, location and degree of the damage if riding is helpful or not. If pain in the hip does not improve during riding, but rather becomes worse, an expert should be consulted.

Shoulder Pain

Shoulder pain often goes hand in hand with the loss of ability to turn the arm to the outside. For riding, this means that the hand can no longer be carried correctly. Prior stretching, slowly and softly moving the shoulder girdle and arm (with the elbow angled to shorten the lever) can have a releasing effect. Properly erecting the body in the TS area is important to give the shoulders a chance to hang freely and unrestrained. In between, one can relieve the arm by letting it hang straight down. At the same time, ride the horse with reins in one hand which is a good way of testing to see if we have ridden the horse correctly so far.

These examples of the major joints are meant to show ways in which to deal with pain. Pain is a kind of police for our body. It indicates that all is not well, and our body is automatically forced to save a particular segment so it can recover. This means that pain has the protective function of saving our body from worse damage. 'Pain, your friend and helper!'

When we accept dealing with pain this way, we find it much easier to handle. The *extent* to which we *perceive pain* can vary greatly. We cannot express it on a scale and by no means can we assess and compare it. While rider X, after having a wisdom-tooth removed, appears the next day for a jumping lesson, rider Y may be prostrate for a whole week. Also, we can influence pain to a great degree psychosomatically. For example, your shoulders are hurting, and all of a sudden you become distracted, or, you are becoming consumed by a task which you manage to execute successfully: pain recedes completely to the background and then often goes as if by magic. On the other hand, when concentrating on pain we just cannot get rid of it. Diverting our thinking is an important factor when dealing with pain.

Breathing can intensify pain or diminish it. Earlier, I described how exhaling is reflexively connected with a release of muscular tension. Pain often occurs because a muscle is cramped. This muscle can then be released by exhaling and pain is diminished as a result. One can definitely worsen pain through hectic and pressed breathing, which, in its turn, often brings on a vicious circle of additional tension and pain (in the areas of shoulders and nape). Breathing and release are important parameters for dealing with pain. When riding, suppling work offers some possibilities for this. Breathing is deepened, the rider concentrates on the horse, is mentally diverted from the pain, the body follows softly and rhythmically the motion of the horse and becomes relaxed and supple. We can further advance this by stretching and letting go of tension. For riding, this would mean that we also execute lengthening movements and stretches on the horse and work only in short reprises; meanwhile we incorporate a break at the walk, put our arms around the horse's neck, allow our arms and legs to hang loosely, and then we start a new work phase.

If you heed these factors, your hobby can

be of significant value for your health and well being.

I did not choose any photos or drawings for illustrating pain. Rather, I would like to encourage you to look again at the illustrations in this book and pay attention to the facial expression. We can almost always deduce from a rider's face if they are feeling good or if they are assuming an unnatural position in a cramped manner.

8.6 Thinking

Who does not know the feeling that the head is in the way? It is when we want something too much, when we want to do it too well and then nothing works out. We are not perfect machines and we cannot switch our physical abilities on and off with the push of a button. When riding, the control of our entire body is required. To concentrate on everything at the same time, is impossible.

When we try to think of everything at once, our head is no longer free to concentrate and react to the actual situation. The difficulty lies in the fact that most of a rider's reactions are executed by automatically-reacting muscles which are not subjected to the conscious range of movement. When trying to execute every little, detailed movement *consciously* we will always be too slow. We will ride well only when we are able to exclude our mind, when we submit ourselves to these automatic reactions and keep the head free for other things. Of course, when in the process of learning a new movement, this is not possible at first. For example, when learning the rising trot, we will have to concentrate on the rhythm and the up and down for so long, until we have experienced the rising trot as a movement. Then it moves into the subconscious, and

we are free to concentrate on something else.

Naturally, there is no way that we can ride without using our mind now and then. Above all, it is important to remain open for any changes on the part of the horse, of ourselves and of our surroundings. Only when perceiving things quickly and surely can we react adequately and correctly. The rider should concentrate in a way that their entire perception remains alert. An experienced trainer once said to me: 'You have to listen to your horse and ask it how it would like to be ridden today!' Then you are able to plan the right work with the right concept for the session. We also need to concentrate on the perception of our own body, when do we sit in front of or behind the motion? Such balance problems must be detected at once in order not to develop a wrong feel for balance. All our sense organs are part of this perception, including the specific reflex organs of the muscles and joints which report on position and tension. When looking down onto our horse in full concentration, we have excluded the eyes this way, one of our most important sense organs.

Freely carrying our head, while looking over the horse's ears and into the direction of movement, is of great importance for proper perception. This is very obvious cross country where it enables us to notice each unevenness of the terrain. When jumping, our eyes are always directed toward the next jump in order to assess the distance correctly. But, in dressage we also need to keep our eyes open, how else can we orient ourselves correctly in the arena? Positive thinking is required when riding. Motivating our thoughts should be essential and a problem should always appear solvable. In our mind we should never anticipate a bad ending.

What a rider thinks tends to happen so

The rider, looking down in full concentration, totally blocks the perception of her own body, thus disturbing her own balance

*Head up,
hands quiet, sternum vertical,
letting go, pushing, legs long,
elastic in the heel, forward,
yielding,
positioning . . .*

Everything at once

negative thoughts are fatal. We should ban them from our mind and concentrate on positive and solvable thoughts. Instead of thinking for example 'My horse is going to throw his head up in the strike off' think 'Next time, I had better keep my outside leg on' or, 'next time, I position Leo better to the inside . . .'

To think of too many things at a time, to have too much on our mind and to block ourselves with de-motivating thoughts are the most typical cases for our head being in the way. In addition to this, there is the so called 'presentation effect'. When we would like to show off something especially well, often nothing works out. To want something too much can block our mind in a way that we can no longer perceive the actual situation. For example, we then ride the flying change although the horse is not properly balanced and the canter is not collected enough, and the change that we wanted to present so badly is a failure.

8.

Think positive!

Finally, we must not underestimate the inside of a human. We bring all our emotions with us onto the horse. All our thoughts and movements are imprinted by our inner situation. There are days when we feel that we could move mountains, we feel in heaven and we ride like we always wished we could ... And on other days, everything goes wrong. It would have been better to not even get on the horse.

The relationship between instructor and student plays an important part. There are instructors who can help us to reach personal record performance. I have an instructor who constantly corrects something, until he finally turns around and mutters 'this is as good as it gets'. With this he shows me that his teaching goals for me are right at the top. This is such a positive motivation for me that I defeat my inner cowardice and struggle through situations I would have otherwise failed in. With such instruction, we sometimes achieve performances we would have never believed possible. Equally, I know of the opposite situation. An instructor once contemptuously accused me of being unable to ride a horse correctly forward and down. All he had to do was appear at the entrance of the indoor school and my horse stuck his nose in the air; not a trace of a stretched topline remained.

The entire surroundings play an important role. Sometimes there is a concentrated atmosphere in the indoor school in which we can ride very successfully. But all it takes is one disturbance and all harmony is gone.

My wish for every rider is to have all their senses open so they can fully perceive their horse; for blissful harmony, the unison between rider and horse, arises from this.

Thank You

This book would have never been finished if so many dear horses and humans had not supported me with infinite and never tiring patience.

My special thanks go to:

- Isabelle, for whom no night was too long, no discussion too much, no expenditure too large, to accompany this book critically and expertly from the first to the last thought, while at the same time taking care of her family, children, horses, move, household and job.
- The publisher who believed me capable of writing this book.
- All my riding instructors, especially my dear parents who helped me experience the complexity of riding in many different ways.
- The physiotherapy instructors who taught me more about riding than they knew themselves.
- The computer specialists who made it possible that I had a fear- and virus-free encounter with this monster by carrying out all the more demanding technical procedures.
- The creative illustrator who enriched the text with illustrations.
- All the riding students who had to translate my concentrated theory into practice – and due to my pestering corrections of certain body segments, always knew exactly what chapter I was working on.
- To all the horses who have helped me and my students to understand bland theory.
- 'Paula', 'Vasall' and 'Bariton' in their main roles of 'reactors' to my seat and seat mistakes and 'Leo', our Shetland pony who made sure that all the horses arrived sane and sound at their photo shoots.
- The Mannheim Riding Club who made the optimal surface and background available for the photo shoots.
- To the brave photographer who never lost his good mood even when it meant moving walls and bringing trees and other background requisites into proper focus, and who never missed the right moment in spite of scorching heat and biting frost.
- To Doris, who voluntarily, reliably and cheerily took over all the thankless jobs in the background.
- To my friends, who made the sign of the cross that this book is finally finished, since they were actively as well as passively affected by the dynamics of the book writing.
- Heike Bean who used her skills to the full to translate the German edition into English. To find someone of her ability and specialist knowledge was a difficult task!
- To the last minute, because if it did not exist, many a thing would never have been finished . . .

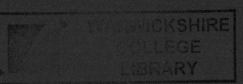